Early Childhood Care and Education
Theory and Practice

ABOUT THE EDITORS

Prerana Mohite is Professor-cum-Dean in the Department of Human Development and Family Studies, Faculty of Family and Community Sciences, The Maharaja Sayajirao University of Baroda. She has vast experience of research and teaching in the field of early childhood care and education. She has been dynamically involved in many regional, national and international programmes for early childhood care and education as well as associated fields.

Larry Prochner is an Associate Professor in the Faculty of Education at the University of Alberta. His research interests include the home/school transitions in preschools in Canada, India and South Africa, and the history of early childhood services with a focus on Canada, Australia and New Zealand. He is co-editor (with N. Howe) of *Early Childhood Education and Care in Canada*, published by the University of British Columbia Press. Also, he is Editor of the Alberta Journal of Educational Research.

EARLY CHILDHOOD CARE AND EDUCATION

Theory and Practice

Edited by

Prerana Mohite

Larry Prochner

CONCEPT PUBLISHING COMPANY, NEW DELHI-110059

Cataloging in Publication Data--DK
Courtesy: D.K. Agencies (P) Ltd. <docinfo@dkagencies.com>

Early childhood care and education : theory and practice / edited by Prerana Mohite, Larry Prochner. -- 1st ed.

p. cm.
Contributed articles.
With special reference to India.
Includes bibliographical references.
Includes index.
ISBN 13: 9788180695353
ISBN 10: 8180695352

1. Child care services. 2. Child care services--India. 3. Early childhood education. 4. Early childhood education--India. I. Mohite, Prerana. II. Prochner, Larry.

DDC 372.210 954 22

ISBN-13: 978-81-8069-535-3 (HB) ISBN-10: 81-8069-535-2 (HB)

First Edition 2009

Published and Printed by
Ashok Kumar Mittal
Concept Publishing Company
A/15-16, Commercial Block, Mohan Garden
New Delhi-110 059 (INDIA)

Phones : 25351460, 25351794
Fax : 091-11-25357109
Email : publishing@conceptpub.com

Foreword

The book has been written by a highly competent and experienced team of professionals led by Prof. Prerana Mohite, Professor and Dean, Department of Human Development and Family Studies, Faculty of Family and Community Sciences, The Maharaja Sayajirao University of Baroda and Prof. Larry Prochner, Faculty of Education, University of Alberta. In this well written book, the contributors have stressed on the importance of play in the early years of a child's development.

In the formative years, pre-school age is a highly impressionable period. In India, there are nearly 150 million children in this category. This signifies the enormous challenge for those engaged in the field of child development, who have the responsibility to ensure attainment of the fullest development potential of children.

Early childhood care and education is among the six goals of "Education for All" that the world is committed to achieving by 2015. Evidence suggests that mental, physical, social, emotional and language development in early years affects learning readiness, academic achievement and overall personality. Play has a great role in contributing to these formative years.

Play encompasses a wide range of activities that generate happiness, enjoyment and fun among children. The thought of play itself creates a sense of joy and pleasure. I wish all children experience this joy and happiness in their lives. This would be possible only if the child care providers are duly sensitized and carry them out in a play-way method. The authors have also been sensitive to the need and contribution of educational programmes for children with special needs.

I take this opportunity to congratulate all the contributors for selecting varied and relevant themes reflecting contemporary thoughts and practices in Early Child Development and giving an opportunity to young students and professionals in the field of early childhood education to take a lead in ensuring that children get their right to education with fun and joy.

Dr. Yogendra N. Mathur
State Representative
UNICEF, Gujarat

Acknowledgements

A lot is happening in the field of *Early Childhood Care and Education* and it has become indeed a vibrant discipline.

This book reflects both, the efforts and programmes of several institutions and scholars.

We have been privileged to put these together in the form of a book.

We would like to put on record our appreciation and acknowledgements to:

- The authors who willingly accepted our invitation to contribute to this volume amidst their busy schedules.
- Concept Publishing Company for their willingness and constant support for publishing this book.
- Ms. Bhavisha Doshi and Ms. Khadija Sodagar, Project Fellows, in UGC Special Assistance Programme of the Human Development and Family Studies for painstakingly and efficiently handling the proof reading as well as providing secretarial support.

Contents

The Contributors

Baljit Kaur: Senior Lecturer, School of Educational Studies & Human Development, College of Education, University of Canterbury, Christchurch, New Zealand. Phone: (64) 3-364-3372; Fax: (64) 3-364-2418.
Email: baljit.kaur@canterbury.ac.nz
Research Interests: Cultural and historical constructions of childhood and early childhood education; early literacy and learning disabilities; children's rights; home school relationships; diversity and schooling; critical ethnography.

Charles M. Super: Professor, Department of Human Development & Family Studies, University of Connecticut, 348 Mansfield Road, Unit 2058, Storrs, Connecticut 06269-2058
Research Interest: Cultural Regulation of Human Development, Particularly Biological, Cognitive, and Emotional Development during Infancy and Childhood; Parental and Professional Ethno theories of Child Development and Behaviour; Interventions to Promote the Physical and Mental Health of Children and Families; Research Methods Appropriate for Comparative and Culturally Based Research.

Jigisha Shastri: Reader, Department of Human Development and Family Studies, Faculty of Family and Community Sciences, The Maharaja Sayajirao University, Vadodara-390002, Gujarat, India
Phone: 0265-786539; Fax: 0265-786539
Email: jigshashastri@yahoo.co.in
Research Interest: Early Childhood Care and Education, Early Literacy, Social Competence, Curriculum for Early Years, Children and Gender, Education in Early Years.

Kishore Shrestha: Lecturer/Research Center for Educational Innovation and Development (CERID), Tribhuvan University, Kathmandu, Nepal
Phone: (977-1)428 6732; Fax: (977-1)427 4224
Email: kishoreshrestha@hotmail.com
Research Interest: She has a wide experience in conducting

experimental and action research projects in the area of child care and education. She is interested in assessing the developmental status of children belonging to various ethnic and diverse cultural settings and looking at how the traditional child care and education practices be strengthened.

Lilian Katz: Professor Emeritus, Early Childhood and Parenting Collaborative Colloege of Education, Universtiy of Illinois at Urbana-Champaign, 29 Children's Research Center, 51 Gerty Dr. MC 671

Email: lgkatz@uiuc.edu

Research Interest: Developmental stages of teachers; mixed-age grouping; teacher-parent relations; teacher education; self-esteem vs. narcissism; gender differences and pedagogy; and dispositions, their development and assessment.

Neerja Sharma: Reader, Department of Human Development and Childhood Studies, Lady Irwin College (University of Delhi), Sikandra Road, New Delhi, India-110001

Telephone: +91-11-23737446/161, 23711222/161

Email: neerja.lic@gmail.com

Research Interests: Childhood disability, families of children with disability, early intervention, guidance and counselling of care-givers; Inclusion and inclusive education; Childhood and adolescent mental health; Adolescent development and identity; Linkage of higher education with basic education; culturally relevant research methods.

Parminder Parmar: Assistant Professor, Department of Human Development and Family Studies, Commonwealth College, Pennsylvania State University, 120 Ridge View Drive, Dunmore, PA 18512 USA

Email: prpl04@psu.edu

Research Interest: Cultural construction of parenting, child development and Education. She has carried out research on children and families in India, Spain, Kuwait, Iran, and the United States. At present she is coordinating a research project on parents' and teachers' role in the development of children across dozen different countries around the world.

Sara Harkness: Professor, Department of Human Development & Family Studies, University of Connecticut, 348 Mansfield Road, Unit 2058, Storrs, Connecticut 06269-2058

Phone: (860) 486-4374; Fax: (860) 486-3452

E-Mail: sara.harkness@uconn.edu

Research Interests: Cultural Structuring of Human Development; Parents Cultural Belief Systems and Parenting; Cognitive, Affective and Social Development in Early Childhood, Child Language Socialization; Theories of Culture and Human Development; Cultural Influences on Health at the Household and Community Levels; Family Policy.

1

Indian Early Childhood Education in Global/Local Context

PRERANA MOHITE and LARRY PROCHNER

Introduction

Playing Across Borders presents a series of essays on 'Early Childhood Care and Development'* (ECCD) services in India that seek to explain the hybrid nature of current practice, using perspectives of history, sociology, psychology, and post-colonial studies. The purpose is to initiate a dialogue on ECCD services that is at once based in local experience, representing Indian objectives, and extended across cultures, including international trends and issues. The focus is on past and present developments in ECCD, and the contributions of Indian and Western ideas to theory and practice in these areas. The essays are grouped around two major themes: the historical sources of ideas, and current issues such as new approaches to curriculum, education for children with special needs and experiments with Indian approaches in other nations. Our goal was to assemble a collection of essays that would appeal to readers, both, inside and outside of India with an interest in

* The term early childhood care and development services was chosen to reflect the range of services that target children in the 0-6 age range, where schooling for children at the upper end of this range is considered to be a component of overall development. The school starting age in India is five or six depending on State regulations.

understanding the global and local conditions that contribute to a culture of ECCD in that nation.

The governments of many countries have voiced support for the development of ECCD services for a variety of economic and humanitarian reasons (Barnett, Escobar, & Escobar, 1990; Schweinhart, Barnes, & Weikart, 1993). In 1990, the Education for All (EFA) movement established ECCD as a key component of an effort to provide basic education for all the world's children, a commitment reiterated over time (Myers, 2000; UNESCO, 1996; UNESCO, 2000). In her capacity as a Managing Director of the World Bank, Ramphele (2002) warned that it is "never too early to become involved but it can easily be too late" (p. vii). As a member of the group of E-9 Countries—nine nations whose combined populations equal more than half the world population—India made progress in the area of ECCD in the 1990s and aimed to expand and improve services in the new century (UNESCO, 2000a; UNESCO, 2000b).

The most effective ECCD programmes support child development in a particular context (Myers, 2000; Young, 2002). Where there is a poor match between the programme and community needs, the programme is unlikely to sustain. While individual nations and communities determine the form and content of services, there is a concern that western ideas and practices are privileged in this regard (Myers, 2000; Prochner & Cleghorn, in press). This situation can result in a poor match between home, the ECCD programme, and later schooling, a problem compounded by the "bureaucratically convenient tendency to extend the same programme to all children (Myers, 2000; p. 22).

More than two decades ago, in the inaugural issue of the journal Early Childhood Research Quarterly, Millie Almy (1993) described uniformity as a feature of early childhood programmes worldwide.

An associate of the Bernad Van Leer Foundation, who has visited early childhood education programmes for poor children in many countries, asked me recently, "Why is it, that whether I go to Kenya, Israel, Bolivia, or Australia, the programmes look and sound so much alike?" (p. 7)

Our delayed response to this question is: In what ways are ECCD services similar and how are they different? Viruru (2001) observed of the situation in India that "very few (if any) would closely resemble the traditional 'Western' conception of what a preschool should look like" (p. 23). Nor does the presence of common features, for example, in room arrangement (activity centres) or the naming of parts of the schedule (free play), mean that they are interpreted in the same way across or within nations (Carlson, 1997; Cleghorn & Prochner, 1997, 2003; Parmar, & Hoot, 1995; Tietze, *et al.*, 1996; Tietze, *et al.*, 1998; Srinivasan & Karlan, 1997; Ulich & Mayr, 1999) recommended: with a gaze affected by expatation, and concentration on the chapters in this volume aim to 'trouble' this representation of ECCD, creating a space for the diversity of approaches to ECCD that exist in India and worldwide.

Early Childhood Development

We believe that child development is subject to cultural influences including childrearing practices (Kagitcibasi, 1996a, 1996b; Mistry & Saraswathi, 2003; Rogoff, 2003). Although there is considerable variation in these practices worldwide, middle-class western childrearing practices that support children within child-focused cultural settings, have dominated research in developmental psychology (Rogoff, 2003). Moreover, although the basic needs of children are generally agreed upon, the way that child care experts describe the best way to meet these needs is sometimes narrowly defined. Brazelton and Greenspan (2000), for example, described seven "irreducible needs of children" and presented strategies for meeting those needs. These included a recommendation that for more than two-thirds of the time in which a preschool-aged child is not in school, parents should be "available to comment on or help with the child's activities, and available for direct, one-to-one interactions" (p.42). Rogoff (2003) refers to these kinds of "child-focused" practices as supporting child development in a particular context (cf. Cannella & Viruru, 2002). In the case of child-focused settings, the practices derive in part from the requirements of schooling, in which children learn to anticipate the structure of classroom interaction (Le Vine, 2003).

Some children are better prepared for schooling based on their experiences at home (Cleghorn & Prochner, 2003). However, instead of considering different home life deficiencies, we believe that the recognition of diverse childrearing practices which support healthy child development creates an opportunity to both, revise schools, and prepare children better for their classroom experiences. It also opens the possibility for an exchange of ideas across cultures.

Participants in different communities may be able to expand their possibilities by cross-fertilization of ideas, by knowing about and mastering forms of communication and learning, which are not indigenous to their own community. There can be mutual enhancement, with some communities learning from others how to engage in the discourse of schooling, for example, and others learning how to engage in skilled observation and coordinated participation in ongoing activities. Rather than looking for 'One Best Way' and regarding cultural patterns as mutually exclusive, each can offer enrichment to others (Rogoff, 2003, p. 356).

Some features of childhood and childrearing in India with relevance to the chapters in this volume are the coexistence of individualist and collectivist orientations in the Indian culture (Sinha & Tripathi, 2003), the significant role of the "joint" family (Tandon, 1981), expectations regarding independence (Joshi & MacLean, 1997) and changes in childrearing practices amongst the growing middle-class (Sharma, 2003; Sinha, 1984).

Early Childhood Programmes

Early childhood programmes reflect a society's values and beliefs concerning children, families and education. "Embedded in communities, nations and cultures, preschools both, reflect and affect social change" (Tobin, Wu, & Davidson, 1989: 2). Cochran's (1993) framework for interpreting the various influences on ECCD policies and programmes are useful for thinking about how this occurs. As Cochran describes, EC programmes are influenced by causal factors subject to mediating influences. For example, a change in traditional family structure (causal factor) creates a need for child care arrangements outside the family circle—in the case of India, the "joint" family. These could be of varying types depending on mediating influences: a cultural belief that child care is the responsibility of parents, and that, in their absence they are responsible for finding and financing substitute care, may result the mushrooming of privately financed programmes outside regulatory control. Historical causal factors related to colonization can be traced in the same manner. For example, the need for a local workforce created a need for schooling in colonial settings. Socio-political and economic ideologies influenced the nature of the policies and programmes, for example, the growth of vocational education or the dominance of English instruction for local populations. This was the case in India during the period of British rule, where education was a mechanism of colonial administration. Colonial systems of schooling were also influenced by local beliefs and norms, which in turn affected the pedagogical approach of EC programmes.

A nation's culture of ECCD is also influenced by global factors. These include the widespread interest in EFA as described at the outset of this chapter, as well as global debates on educational issues such as those identified by Anderson-Levitt (2003), whether for example, should schooling be student-centred or content-centred? (p. 9). We agree with Anderson-Levitt that systems of schooling are rarely compartmentalised strictly; More of ten than not they include multiple elements. For example reforms can be student-centred but also content centred. Examples of other reform debates, more particular to EC programmes, are: How can they be present-oriented but also look to the future? How can they have a paediatric focus but also be concerned with pedagogy? How can they be the responsibility of the family but also involve the State? And, in relation to India, as described above, how can they be individualist but also collectivist in their orientation?

The Transfer of Educational Ideas

'I have no difficulty in agreeing with the scientific views of Madame Montessori. However, if they are propagated in their Western garb in Indian villages, they are more likely to prove useless and might even prove harmful, because in that grab they will be too expensive for Indian villages and ill-adapted to the village atmosphere.' (Gandhi, 1945: 370-71)

The transfer of educational ideas across borders has a long history, and in the case of early childhood education, it is closely related to nineteenth century colonial expansion in which successive models of early childhood education were exported around the British Empire (Prochner & Cleghorn, in press). Phillips & Ochs (2003) described a four-phase model of policy borrowing in education: (i) cross-national attraction, (ii) decision, (iii) implementation, and (iv) internalization/indigenization. In the case of India as in Africa, the initial attraction and decision occurred through a mix of internal and external influences weighted "to support the economic and political motives of the colonial powers" (Phillips & Ochs: 458). As the essays in this volume demonstrate, EC programmes in India with Western origins are now mostly at the internalization/indigenization phase of development. However, the essays also make clear that the colonial legacy has had mixed benefits. According to a UNESCO report at the end of the 1970s:

> 'Almost all [the programmes] draw their inspiration from Western models, and adhere to systems like the Montessorian, Froebelian, or more eclectic "nursery" systems. This has affected the nature of the material and methods used. Instruction in English language is often a matter of prestige. A common and disturbing trend in all the countries is the increasing stress, often in response to parental pressure on early introduction to formal learning and preparatory work for literacy, amounting to direct instruction of the 3 Rs.' (UNESCO, 1979: 7-8).

The report continued by drawing attention to conflicts between theory and practice:

> 'Theoretical conflicts are reflected visibly at the teaching/learning level. There may be talk of free choice of activity, but in remote rural settings, there are often, in practice, no materials for the children to play with. There may be stress on discussion, individual choice, group problem-solving, democratic procedures and other inter-personal interactions, but in practice, the atmosphere may be authoritarian, with the teacher leading a tightly controlled schedule of group activities.' (UNESCO, 1979: 11)

A similar situation was noted ten years later:

> 'These approaches [to ECE], sometimes complementary and sometimes conflicting, are broadly based on the experiences of developed countries. ... Much of the knowledge upon which programme designs are based, and many of the programme models used have their origin in the West, or are based on narrow, out-moded, or culturally inappropriate views of early childhood development.' (UNESCO, 1988: 3-4)

And still, in 2002, Kaul (2002) urged Indian educators "to revisit the ECCD and primary curriculum from the perspective of including into the developmental objectives, the cultural values and behavioural practices that are a part of the Indian tradition" (p. 31). However, while the export of play-based methodologies from the West continues and policy-makers often endorse learning through play, there is considerable variation in the way the methods are understood and employed (see chapter by Prochner in this volume). Educational policy regarding EC programmes is more uniform than practice (Ramirez, 2003).

Early Childhood Development and Education in India

The essays included in this book cover a varied range and reflect several current global trends and concerns referred to earlier.

Chapter one on playway in India explores the idea of playway in Indian preschools. It describes how playway is conceived and implemented in different types of early childhood programmes. More often than not, the programme draws ideas from western theories and models with adaptation to local culture. The pre-primary programme (Dakshinamurty Bal Mandir) in Bhavnagar clearly demonstrates how it is rooted in Montessorian theory. In fact, today in India, it is probably the only programme based on Montessori's theory adapted to Indian culture.

On the other hand, playway is conceived and implemented very differently in the ICDS preschool programmes that encompass almost 400,000 preschool centres. In the ICDS, the preschool programme is planned as one of the essential services for poor children. It differs significantly from the rest of the preschools on the count that it totally lacks the 'formal readiness to school' component.

ECCE and playway in private sector are concentrated on "formal teaching" ranging from the most direct and formal to the indirect and informal programmes of readiness. In fact, one of the disturbing issues and concerns of early childhood educators in India is the large growth of unregulated private schools that are comparable to "teaching shops". The chapter vividly brings out the complex shades in which playway is conceptualized and implemented in various preschool institutions/centres in India.

The essay draws out the criticality of playway in India in relation to western theories of play. Although the focus of the chapter is on conceptions and practice of "playway" in Indian preschools, the author situates it in the context of global trends and thinking on play based education. In a nutshell, the chapter engages in tracing theoretical roots of play as postulated by western as well as Indian educators such as Comenius, Pestalozzi, Froeble, Montessori and Gandhi. Taking off from such theoretical background, the chapter effectively refers to real situations and practices in Indian preschools, private as well as major national programmes like the ICDS. The differences in private and public preschool sectors in India is clearly culled out which raises critical issues about the delivery of preschool services. The chapter sets an appropriate setting and context for the remaining chapters that illustrate the wide range of preschool programmes offered in India at various levels.

Sharma's essay on play concerns itself with 'Children with Special Needs'. It discusses play in relation to disabilities of various types, for instance, intellectual, visual and language. The chapter also delves into the cultural-familial construction of play and disability. Through systematic documentation of specific research studies related to play experience of the child with special needs, the author points out how play in India is person focused rather than object focused. Since "Inclusion and mainstreaming" are the current emphasis in ECCE in India, this essay provides a useful direction in planning an integrated (inclusive) programme for children with special needs.

The essay on an Indian model of Early Childhood Care and Education in a Nepalese context concerns itself with services and management of ECCE in India and Nepal. By examining Integrated Child Development Services in India, one of the largest child development programmes in the world, the chapter attempts to understand the management and implementation of a large scale ECCE Programme in developing countries. In doing so, it critically examines important dimensions of the ICDS programme as well as its constraints. The important engagement of this essay is to view an Indian experience critically while drawing out implications for Nepal. The chapter reveals that although the delivery and implementation of the ICDS have several serious lacunae and constraints, the strength of the programme is in its effective conceptualization of how a viable ECCE programme can be planned and executed in a large, developing country.

Taking a cross cultural perspective, the essay on cultural diversity in parental ethno-theories on play and learning questions the universality and homogeneity of children's play across cultures and subcultures. The authors bring in theoretical conceptions and researches from developmental psychology to demonstrate how play and learning are embedded in a cultural context.

The essay on project approach in early childhood programmes is an illustration of using this approach in an Indian preschool. The setting is a lab preschool of the Department of Human Development and Family Studies, where the project approach recommended by Helm and Katz (2002) was implemented. The chapter elaborately presents the systematic implementation of this approach in an Indian setting. In light of the learning outcome of children at the completion of the project implementation, the author critically discuss its implications and application in the Indian cultural context.

The last chapter by Baljit Kaur lives up to its title and leapfrogs early childhood education in India through a century. The major developments in ECCE through various commissions, official documents, pioneering efforts of Indian as well as European educators help in getting an overview of ECCE in India from 1830s to 1940s. The author's own interpretation and analysis of various reports and documents provide an effective perspective on how ECCE has emerged in India. Her interviews with several early childhood educators provide a rich data source on thoughts and ideas not documented yet. In a way, this chapter's merit and contribution is in documenting a history of ECCE in India. While the information has been available in several documents and books, the strength of the chapter is in providing a good understanding of this information as a significant basis for a historical account.

In summing, this series of essays on Early Childhood Care and Education services in India reveals certain striking features of the current scenario. The private sector (catering to middle and upper middle class) represents the didactic, predominantly verbal, group oriented and scholastic nature of ECCE programmes. The public sector (typically known as Government schools) is characterized by rigid, often inappropriate curriculum, poor pedagogy and poor learning.

The government's main concern and investment in ECCE is service delivery oriented, clearly visible in ICDS, which is soon to be universalized. There are, in addition, few innovative and effective ECCE programmes, that may be rooted in western theories, but are contextualized meaningfully in the local culture. Further, there are also some programmes that are "contemporary" in their approach to curriculum pedagogy, grounded in sound theories and well adapted to the Indian culture.

Each essay raises very pertinent issues that must be addressed when viewed against the backdrop of global trends in ECCE.

Some common themes emerging through the essays can be summarized as follows:

- The conception and ideological sources of varied ECCE programmes in India are rooted in Western theories as well as ideas of Indian educators/philosophers. A large number of ECCE programmes are adaptations of western models to local cultural settings. This reflects an effort to integrate global developments and trends in early childhood thinking as well as practices.
- There is an emerging trend to consider parental participation much beyond "attending parents' meeting". The essay on ethno-theories of parents in play and learning evidences this emerging trend.
- There is a reiteration of play and playway for children with special needs. A significant response that is highlighted is the distinct nature and pattern of play in India and the west. In India, play is rooted in "persons" unlike in western world where 'objects' dominate.
- The ICDS—though the largest ECCE programme in the world, is by no means a totally successful programme. Yet, the Indian Government continues its salient efforts to universalize it and to strike a balance between quantitative expansion and maintaining minimum quality. As reflected in the chapter by Shrestha, ICDS has the potential to become a model of ECCE service delivery for developing countries.

In closing one may state that the wide ranging ECCE programmes and services in India mirror the developmental status and nature of the contemporary Indian context, each representing a relevant section and ideology of society and community (or of stakeholders). These are, at times complementary and at times contradictory.

Also, one may often observe a mismatch between the ideology and theory behind the programme and the actual practices. Based on the current situation and renewed interest in ECCE, it may be concluded that among policy makers, practitioners and consumers of ECCE, there is an understanding of global developments and trends, with a sincere attempt to contextualize these in the local culture. One hopes that the two will converge over time leading to ECCE programmes that are culturally sensitive and relevant.

REFERENCES

Anderson-Levitt, K. (2003). A world culture of schooling? In K. Anderson-Levitt (Ed.), *Local meanings, global schooling: Anthropology and world culture theory* (pp. 1-27). New York: Palgrave Macmillan.

Barnett, W., Escobar, S., & Escobar, C. (1990). Economic costs and benefits of early intervention. In S.J. Meisels & J.P. Shonkoff (Eds.), *Handbook of early childhood intervention* (pp. 560-582). New York: Cambridge University Press.

Brazelthon, T.B. & Greenspan, S.I (2000). *The irreducible needs of children: What every child must have to grow, learn, and flourish.* Cambridge, MA: Perseus.

Cannella, G.S. & Viruru, R. (2002). *(Euro-American construction of) education (and adults) around the world: A postcolonial critique.* G.S. Cannella & J. Kincheloe (Eds.)

Carlson, H.L. (1997) Early Childhood education in societal context: teachers in three countries speak about early childhood education. *Early Education and Development*, 8(2), 169-86.

Cleghorn, A. & Prochner, L. (1997). Early Childhood education in Zimbabwe: Recent trends and prospects. *Early Education and Development*, 8(3), 339-352. *Special Issue*: Children, families, and change: International Perspectives.

Cleghorn, A. & Prochner, L. (2003). Contrasting visions of childhood: Examples from settings in India and Zimbabwe. *Journal of Early Childhood Research*, 1(2), 131-153.

Cochran, M. (1990). Public child care, culture, and society: Crosscutting themes. In M. Cochran (Ed.), *International handbook of child care policies and programs* (pp. 627-58).

Gandhi, M.K. (Apr. 12, 1945). Letter to S. Sarabhai. (CW 71). In *Gandhi on education.*

Joshi, M. & MacLean, M. (1997). Maternal expectations of child development in India, Japan, and England. *Journal of Cross-Cultural Psychology*. 28(2), 219-234.

Kagitcibasi, C. (1996a). Cross-cultural psychology and development. In J. Pandey & D. Sinha (Eds), *Asian contributions to cross-cultural psychology* (pp. 42-49). New Delhi: Sage.

Kagitcibasi, C. (1996b). Family and human development across cultures: A view from the other side. Mahwah, NJ: Erlbaum.

Kidworld: Childhood studies, global perspectives, and education (pp. 197-243). New York: P. Lang.

Learning and educational change. Hong Kong: Comparative Education Research Centre.

LeVine, R.A. (2003). Childhood socialization: Comparative studies of parenting.

Mistry, J. & Saraswathi, T.S. (2003). The cultural context of child development. In R.M. Lerner & A.M. Easterbrooks, M. Ann (Eds) *Handbook of psychology: Developmental psychology*, Vol. 6 (pp. 267-291). New York: John Wiley & Sons.

Myers, R.G. (2000). *Early childhood development and care. Education for All 2000 assessment.* Thematic studies. Paris: United Nations Educational, Scientific and Cultural Organization.

New Delhi: National Council for Teacher Education.

Parmar, R.S., & Hoot, J.L. (1995). International Perspectives on Developmentally Appropriate Practices. *Contemporary Education*, 66(3), 150-53.

Phillips, D., & Ochs, K. (2003). Processes of policy borrowing in education: Some explanatory and analytical devices. *Comparative Education*, 39(4), 451-461.

Practitioners' attitudes and practice. *International Journal of Early Years Education*, 7(1), 25-37.

Prochner, L. & Cleghorn, A. (in press). Cross-cultural research as a lens on early childhood thought and practice. In V. Pacini-Ketchabaw & A. Pence (Eds.), *Research connections 10: Reconceptualizing early childhood and development*. Ottawa: Canadian Child Care Federation.

Ramphele, M. (2002). Foreword. In World Bank, From early childhood development to human development: Investing in our children's future. Washington: World Bank.

Rogoff, B. (2003). *The cultural nature of human development*. New York: Oxford University Press.

Schweinhart, L., Barnes, H., & Weikart, D. (1993). *Significant benefits: The High/Scope Perry Preschool Study though age 27*. Ypsilanti, MI: High/Scope Press.

Sharma, D. (2003). *Childhood, family and sociocultural change in India—Reinterpreting the inner world.* Oxford: Oxford University Press.

Sinha, D. (1984). Some recent changes in the Indian family and their implications for socialization. *Indian journal of Social Work.* 45(3), 271-286.

Sinha, D. & Tripathi, R.C. (2003). Individualism in a collectivist culture: A case of coexistence of opposites. In T.S. Saraswathi (Ed.) *Cross-cultural perspectives in human development: Theory, research, and applications* (pp. 192-210). New Delhi: Sage.

Srinivasan, B., Karlan, G.R. (1997). Culturally responsive early intervention programs: Issues in India. *International Journal of Disability, Development and Education*, 44(4), 367-85.

Tandon, T. (1981). Process of transmission of values in the Indian child. In D. Sinha (Ed.), *Socialization of the Indian Child* (pp. 11-29). New Delhi: Concept.

Tietze, W., Bairrao, J., Leal, T., Rossbach, H.G. (1998). Assessing Quality Characteristics of Center-Based Early Childhood Environments in Germany and Portugal: A Cross-National Study. *European Journal of Psychology of Education*, 13(2), 283-98.

Tietze, W., Cryer, D., Bairrao, J., Palacios, J., & Wetzel, G. (1996). Comparisons of observed process quality in early child care and education programs in five countries. *Early Childhood Research Quarterly*. 11(4), 447-75.

Tobin, J., Wu, D., & Davidson. D. (1989). *Preschool in three cultures: Japan, China and United States*, New Haven, CT: Yale University Press.

Ulich, M. & Mayr, T. (1999). *Observing children in German day care centres*.

United Nations Educational, Scientific and Cultural Organization. (2000a) *The Dakar Framework for Action. Education for All: Meeting our collective Commitments*, adopted by the World Education Forum, Dakar, Senegal, 26-28 April 2000. Paris: Author.

United Nations Educational, Scientific and Cultural Organization.

(2000b). *Education for All: The year 2000 assessment report*, India. Paris: Author.

United Nations Educational, Scientific, and Cultural Organization. (1996). *Education for All, Achieving the Goal: Statistical Document*. Mid-Decade Meeting of the International Consultative forum on Education for All, 16-19 June 1996. Amman, Jordan. Paris: Author.

Viruru, R. (2001). *Early Childhood education: Postcolonial perspectives from India*. New Delhi: Sage.

Westport, CT: *Greenwood*.

2

Playway in India

LARRY PROCHNER

This chapter explores the idea of playway[1] in preschool programs in India and the concurrent trend towards more formal instruction. In particular, it examines the relation of Western play theory to the Indian version of play-based education called playway. Although playway is often associated with Indian pre-schools, its practice is not widespread. The chapter begins by briefly describing the westernized approach to play-based preschool education in India.

Three presuppositions frame the discussion. The first is that childhood is a social construction. By this we mean that childhood is a category of human development based on culturally and historically situated ideas (Cunningham, 1996: James and Prout, 1990: James *et al.*, 1998). The second is that the services a society provides for children and families, for example, preschool education and out of home child care, are governed in part by these particular representations of childhood (Cannella, 1997: Silin, 1995). The third is that the globalized and universalised ideas concerning childhood and early childhood education, compete with locally conceived ideas and services. Whereas research in developmental psychology has shown that there are few universal principles of development (Burman, 1994: Fox and Prilleltensky, 1997: Ogbu, 1981), globalization emphasizes the common experience of childhood and flattens differences. Some experiences are taken to have a meaning that transcends culture, for example, play. Understanding of children's play is constructed on a tableau of ideas on childhood and childrearing (Roopanarine et al., 1994). In light of the diversity of the experiences of childhood, a pedagogical approach that hinges on a single definition of play is not tenable.

Local ideas about play in early childhood settings are created out of the tension between culturally and historically situated beliefs and international ideas. In the field of preschool education, these international ideas have been dominated by Western theory, which has historically assigned play a privileged role. These theories are identified with nineteenth and twentieth century educators such as Froebel, Montessori and Dewey, and psychologists such as Freud, Vygotsky and Piaget. Bennett *et al.* (1997) referred to this "ideological, philosophical and educational tradition" as the "nursery inheritance". While play does not mean the same thing in each case (Saracho and Spode, 1998), play-based approach is at the opposite end of the continuum from formal instruction. While the latter is mechanical, de-contextualized and adult-centred (developmentally inappropriate), play-based education is natural, responsive to context and child-centred (developmentally appropriate). Western play-based approaches were favoured by early childhood education experts, and recommended for all children regardless of social class.

Since the Head Start studies in the United States of America in the 1960s and 1970s, adult-centered approaches to early education have often been associated with the scripted instruction of the behaviourist model (Bereiter and Engelmann, 1966)-an experience that can leave children with "serious negative emotional residue" (Schweinhart and Weikart, 1998: 58). Formal early education was called "mis-education" by Elkind (1988). He charged that parents who enrolled their children in such programs "engage in practices that are more reflective of parental ego than of parental need" (Elkind, 1988: xiv). My position, however, is that the debate over the value of play *versus* other forms of learning in early childhood programs is value-laden. Western preschools emphasize autonomy and self direction (Cannella, 1997; Jipson, 1991; Tobin *et al.*, 1989).

They aim to meet the "democratic ideal" and are "production oriented" (Woodhead, 1996:91). A play-based approach centring on children's activity is seen as a way to meet these goals. Conversely, formal instruction in preschool is demonized as a threat to socialization for citizenship in a democracy (Greenberg, 1990, 1992). Concern over the rising tide of academic instruction in preschools was a factor in the creation of principles of developmentally appropriate practice (DAP) by the National Association for the Education of Young Children (Breadkamp and Copple, 1996). Bredkamp (1998: 186) wrote that "the document (Developmentally Appropriate Practice in Early Childhood Programmes) is a political statement about what NAEYC and its members think constitutes the good life for children". Nonetheless, there have been attempts to export a single version of the good life to children elsewhere in the world. An example is the Step by Step[2] programme funded by financier George Soros through the Open Society Institute, and recently reported in on popular publications for early childhood educators in the United States of America (Ford and Coughlin, 1999: Seefeldt and Galper, 1998).

Yet, the practice of preschool is often at odds with expert advice. Everyday, hundreds of thousands of children set off for preschool to learn the basics of literacy and numeracy using rote learning strategies such as memorization and group drill, in countries as diverse as India, Kenya, Nigeria, Taiwan and Thailand (Olmsted and Weikart, 1989, Sestini, 1985; Woodill *et al.*, 1992). Said (1997) wrote about the gap between expert advice and preschool practice in Kenya. Instead of encouraging children to ask and answer questions, or attempting to interact with the children as much as possible, teachers spend a lot of time keeping children quiet and reducing them. This behaviour on the part of the teacher instils fear in the children and destroys their confidence. Teachers run most preschools in Kenya with firm ideas on discipline and behaviour. They have large enrolments, often with one class of up to 40 children, and have no opportunities to discover and explore or even move around the room. It might be concluded from this state of affairs that Kenyan preschools are dismal institutions that prepare children for the worst aspects of a test-driven, competitive education system. However, such a critique would depend on a particular construction of childhood, and of the appropriate relationship between children and adults in an educational setting. We do not mean to make judgment that Kenyan preschools of the type described above are 'appropriate', rather, that an assessment should consider multiple factors. Examples include cultural values regarding such issues as crowding (Liddell and Kruger, 1987, 1989), the amount and type of play materials (Liddell, 1995, Woodhead, 1996), ideas concerning discipline and child-adult interaction, and the relation between preschools and social class (Gakura, 1992).

The Case of India

The nations of the world have been categorized according to their level of industrialization and quality of life variables (industrialized, developing and least developed). India is both an industrial giant and technological leader, and a developing nation. In his speech on the occasion of India's 50th Republic Day (Schmetzer, 2000), K. R. Narayanan, the President of India, spoke of two Indias, "We have one of the world's largest reservoirs of technical personnel but also the world's largest number of illiterates; the world's largest middle class, but also the largest number below the poverty line, and the largest number of children suffering from malnutrition" (Schmetzer: B6). In 2000, India had an infant mortality rate of 70 per 1,000 live births, 2,400,000 deaths of children under the age of 5, and an adult literacy rate of 71 per cent for males, and 44 per cent for females (United Nations Children's Fund, 2001a). India was ranked 128th of 174 countries on the United Nation's Human Development Index, just below Iraq and Lesotho (United Nations Development Programme, 2000). However, historical statistics point to significant social gains in India. In 1983, the infant mortality rate was 104.9 per 1,000 live births (National Institute of Public Cooperation and Child Development, 1997). The infant mortality rate in the year 2000 represented a decrease of 66 per cent over the previous decade. However, lowered infant mortality rate is not limited to India. Vaccination, feeding and health programmes for pregnant women and young children have changed the focus of agencies such as the United Nation's Children's Fund from child survival to child development (United Nation's Children's Fund, 1996). As Myers (1992: xviii) wrote: "12 of every 13 children born in 1991 will live to see their first birthday."[3] The question posed by Myers was "What will happen to the 'twelve who survive'?" India is a particularly compelling case in which to consider this question.

Myers conceded that he was "not concerned with problems of the middle or upper classes", whether they be found in India or Sweden, even though some of these children may be at risk of a distorted and unhealthy development resulting from over-indulgence or from other conditions increasingly present among 'favoured' social groups: (1992: xxi). However, the problems created by a pressurized preschool experience are of great concern in India for the general public (Viruru, 1998) as well as experts (Verma in Bhavnagri, 1995). Private preschools are over subscribed, and the competition for admission in the lead schools is intense, with as many as 300 children competing for a single opening. This phenomenon is not limited to the elite. A bourgeois revolution in India has resulted in the growth of the consumer class and more parents who are able to purchase their children a preschool experience (Stein, 1993). A study in the state of Tamil Nadu revealed that even parents from low-income communities in urban areas sought out private preschools for their children once they reached four years of age. (M.S. Swaminathan Research Foundation, 2000).

An important context for preschool in India is primary school. Primary school enrolment increased over the past decade to reach 109,044,000 in 1995 (United Nations Educational, Scientific, and Cultural Organization, 1996). However, the drop-out rate continued to be very high. In the state of Gujarat, one quarter of children do not enrol in school at all. Of those that enrol, 60 per cent leave after the first grade, and 40 per cent of the remaining students leave school before the end of grade four. The reasons for not enrolling or leaving school include poverty and economic conditions, including the need for children's labour, which in the case of girls, is often related to looking after younger siblings. Other reasons are the poor quality of the school experience and the lack of relevance of school learning to children's lives. Overcrowding and shortage of textbooks are part of the normal school experience for most children. The average pupil to teacher ratio in India is 64:1 (United Nations Educational, Scientific, and Cultural Organization, 1996). The high ratio is supported by adult-centered teaching methods that leave little room for learning through play. As one commentator observed, given the state of school infrastructure and the poor quality of instruction, rather than asking the question of why children do not come to school, we should perhaps ask the question why they come to school in spite of the poor infrastructure and unattractive ways of teaching (Sinha, 1998: 4).

A number of global factors have drawn attention to improving the quality and increasing the quantity of preschool and primary education. The right to education is part of the Universal Declaration of Human Rights (Article 26) as well as the Convention on the Rights of the Child (Article 28). Preschool education was "one of the main pillars of the Education for All movement" (Early Childhood Programmers', 1997: 41) supported by the United Nations Development Programme, United Nations Educational, Scientific, and Cultural Organization, United Nation's Children's Fund, and the World Bank. Over time, the emphasis of the Education for All movement has shifted from the number of children attending school to what they are learning and the quality of their experiences. Improvements in preschools were viewed as a starting point for more general reforms in curriculum and teaching in primary schools. A main area of reform is in the introduction of play way in the early years. However, informal approaches in preschools have generally been overwhelmed by the competitive school context in both, the public and private sectors. Moreover, because school is the ideological context for preschools, there is focus on teaching rather than child development (Swaminathan, 1993).

The Roots of Playway

As discussed in the chapter by Kaur in this volume, European-style preschool programmes were introduced into India in small numbers in the early years of the 19th century as philanthropic and missionary efforts. Over time, Western programmes were adapted according to Indian ideas on pre-primary education and on education in general, thus laying the foundation for the Indian approach to play-based education. The educational ideas of Mohandas K. Gandhi and Rabindranath Tagore are the two most frequently cited influences on preschool education in modern India. Both were advocates of universal education, basic education and education with a practical basis that focused on the development of the whole child (Cenkner, 1994). Tagore promoted a view of the natural child and the corrupting influence of formal schooling (Mani, 1961). He believed that nature was the best teacher, and under the age of seven, children were to learn through natural objects. Children were viewed as having a natural gift to learn, but schools alienated them from this gift by enforcing conformity. Unlike adults, children had minds that were free and creative. The ideal school recognized this and provided activities that focused on music, art and poetry, and children's happiness. This latter emphasis is continued in the spirit of current educational reforms at the pre-primary and primary levels in India, which aim to make learning joyful (the 'joyful learning' or Tarang approach).

One historian described Gandhi as a child centered idealist, who believed that the body and the spirit should be educated as one (Mani, 1961). For Gandhi, education was meant to be free and compulsory, conducted through the learning of craft, and self-supporting through the sale of crafts made by students. Industrial training, in which both boys and girls were taught a handicraft, was linked to spiritual training. Literacy and book learning was not emphasized. Education was to be conducted in the vernacular, and stress the ideal of citizenship in a free India. The four stages of Gandhi's plan were: (i) education through parents and the community (from conception to 2-and-one-half); (ii) pre-basic education conducted by school teachers, at home and by the community; (iii) basic education from age 7 to 15; and (iv) post-basic education, or education for self sufficiency, in late-adolescence. Pre-basic education was broken down into two sub-stages; from two a-half to four education was through play and group activities; from four to seven years of age, children engaged in more purposeful activities. Thus, pre-basic education is interpreted as support for pre-primary or preschool education. In pre-basic education, teaching had the nurturing role of a mother to educate the spirit and not use the mind and body.

The importance of a child's mother as the first and most important teacher of educating the child, was part of the European philosophy of early education expressed in the writings of Johann Amos Comenius, Johann Pestalozzi and Friedrich Froebel. Nineteenth century naturalistic theories of education emphasized hands-on experience and took a dim view of formal instruction. The Finnish educator Uno Cygnaeus extended Forebel's idea of handwork in the kindergarten to include real-world manual training in such crafts as carpentry and basket weaving. The importance of activity and sensory-based learning found expression in the handicraft education movement in Europe, and later, as part of the doctrine of the New Education movement. However, most sources indicate that while Indian educational reformers such as Gandhi and Tagore were aware of these ideas in the West, it merely reinforced what had been arrived at independently in an Indian context.

Two schools established along Frobelian and Montessori lines in the early decades of the 20th Century show the meeting of Indian and Western ideas. The Children's Garden School, one of the two schools was founded by Ellen Sharma and her husband, Dr. V.N. Sharma, in 1936. Ellen Sharma was a European with master's degree in the humanities and education. Her approach incorporated aspects of Froebel and Montessori in an Indian social and cultural context. According to a long time teacher at her school, this meant a greater focus on "group education" than on individuals, and the use of local materials for teaching aids (Rajalakshmi, no date: 20). Materials included Montessori-influenced items, such as cylinders, colour cards and geometrical insets, along with indigenous materials such as seeds for tracing the outlines of designs and letters (*rangoli*). In all aspects of the curriculum there was a focus on practical work, learning by doing. Learning through repetition and self effort (Rajalakshmi, 1998). The pre-primary school (Bal Mandir) in Bhavnagar was also influenced by Maria Montessori, the foreign educator most often associated with Indian preschools. Much of the early interest in Montessori was centered in the state of Gujarat (then part of Maharashtra). In 1915, a Montessori school was established near Vadodara, (Murlidharan and Kaul, 1993) and in 1920, Gijubhai Badheka, among others, opened the Bal Mandir at Bhavnagar. Badheka adapted Montessori materials and methods to suit Indian conditions (Murlidharan and Kaul: 26). The Bal Mandir incorporated Western and Indian educational ideas in a Hindu Nationalist context. Thus, there was considerable emphasis on religion (Hinduism), language (Gujarati) and culture (traditional music, art, dance), along with Montessori materials and activities. Today, the Bal Mandir is part of a larger educational institution called Shri Dakshinamurty Vidyarthi Bhavan, which includes a primary and secondary school, as well as a pre-primary teacher's training college (Shri Dakshinamurty Vidyarthi Bhavan, no date). Altogether, the institution has about 2,600 students, with 600 of them enrolled in the Bal Mandir.

Despite their having some fundamental differences, the Children's Garden and the Bal Mandir have some aspects in common. Both offer children a structured learning environment in which free play in both, the Western sense and as imagined by Tagore (play that children initiate and control) have a minimal role. Groups in both preschools are large and led by a single teacher and a helper or intern, a situation that is only partly due to the number of children that need to be served, or to economic considerations. At the Children's Garden, the director linked the move to larger group sizes in recent times to the continued process of indigenization of preschool education, as well as finances.

There tends to be a high proportion of teacher directed activities in Indian preschools, including whole group games in which children follow a leader, as observed by Roopnarine, *et al.* (1994). Individual and small group activities may involve flash cards, lotto games and work sheets offering practice on number and reading problems. Indian values of conformity and interdependence are reflected in preschools. "As against the independent pluralistic society of the West, India is an interdependent society. Feelings of mutual care and interdependence are culturally reinforced, and individuality and competition is discouraged" (Bhogle, 1999: 281). A supervisor of a university laboratory nursery school, accustomed to the reaction of Western visitors to the degree of teacher direction in preschools, wrote that,

> 'Teacher interaction and mediation may seem like teacher domination, especially compared to some Western schools or visitors from a different culture. But, a balance of giving children a chance to explore by themselves, interact with other children and material, and teachers providing assistance in achieving a task, giving information, questioning and talking does seem to help the children.' (Shastri, 1997: 12).

The approach to play in settings associated with academic child study, such as the laboratory nursery school, is more similar to Western programmes than the Children's Garden and Bal Mandir. The Chetan Balwadi is the laboratory preschool at the Department of Human Development and Family Studies, Maharaja Sayajirao University of Baroda in Gujarat State. It was established in the American home economics tradition of child study in 1949 (Faculty of Home Science, 1999, Saraswathi *et al.*, 1988). The founders of the laboratory preschool set out to create an alternative to the Montessori dominated preschools of the time that were considered overly rigid. "The play method, based on child development research and the nursery school movement, was virtually unknown" (Verma cited in Bhavnagri, 1995: 157). Hallmarks of this new approach were low ratios of teachers to children, more small group activities, and more free play and child-initiated activities. The role of children's activity and interaction in learning was stressed. This more Westernized approach to playway was promoted by the Indian Association for Preschool Education, and the two main national-level research and training institutions concerned with preschool education (the National Institute for Public Cooperation and Child Development, and the National Council for Education Research and Training). As a theoretical approach, child-centred playway has been sustained through the efforts of experts at universities and research institutions, and officials in government agencies responsible for preschool education. However, it is not widely practiced, and playway in preschools, in whatever form, is an exception rather than the rule. This fact is noted in almost all commentaries on preschool education in India (see, for example, Kaul, 1992).

Playway in Public Sector Preschools

Preschool services are provided by a wide range of government and voluntary agencies in India. The Government of India's Integrated Child Development Services (ICDS)[4] includes more than 350,000 preschool centres (anganwadis), serving approximately 10 million children in the age group 3 to 6. Started in 1975, the ICDS is the largest Early Childhood Care and Education programme in the world. The objectives of the ICDS are comprehensive, and they include promotion of child and maternal health (immunization, health checkups, referral services, treatment of minor illnesses), nutrition (supplementary feeding, growth monitoring and promotion, nutrition and health education), and preschool education for children aged three to six (Department of Women and Child Development, 1995). The programme has been very successful in health promotion, particularly through its immunization and feeding programmes. However, an ongoing concern has been the quality of preschool education in the anganwadis.

In the early years of the ICDS, preschool education played a secondary role to the feeding and vaccination programmes, in a pattern consistent with child survival programmes of the time. In the late 1990s, the ICDS underwent a transition to incorporate child care and greater attention to preschool education. According to a Department of Women and Child Development publication, "the early childhood care and preschool education component of the ICDS may well be considered the backbone of the ICDS programme, since all its services essentially converge on the anganwadi. This is also the most joyful playway daily activity, visibly sustained for three hours a day" (Department of Women and Child Development, 1995: 9).

However, the delivery of playway was limited by the resources of the anganwadis and the skills and training of the anganwadi workers. A difference in viewpoint between those in charge of curriculum and training who promoted playway, and parents and community members who sometimes favoured the opposite, namely, a formal school-like approach to literacy and numeracy education in the early years also affected the delivery of playway. The out-right neglect of playway in the first decade of the ICDS was highlighted in the first of the two major reviews of the service by the National Institute of Public Co-operation and Child Development. Adarsh Sharma, who directed both studies, described a typical anganwadi in the 1987 report.

'All the anganwadis' by and large looked alike in their setup. Faded charts of birds, animals, fruits, alphabets and numbers adorned the walls. In most cases, these were stuck far above the eye level of children... Their daily routine included teaching of numbers through rote method. The anganwadi was turned into a primary school, the concept of non-formal preschool education was obviously not followed or implemented as envisaged in this scheme.... The investigation reported that only approximately 26-30 percent of anganwadi children looked happy, involved and absorbed in the ongoing activities. An equally small proportion of the anganwadi workers permitted children freedom of movement to explore surroundings. The children were found seated in rows, one behind the other, unable to look at each other. The anganwadi workers were usually seated on a chair with a table in front of the class far away and far too high for establishing eye contact with the children. Discipline was enforced strictly, making children epitomes of conformist behaviour' (Sharma, 1987: 57-59).

The 1987 study did not measure the effect of preschool education on children's learning. A 1992 study compared children who had attended an anganwadi and a control group of children with no preschool experience (National Institute of Public Cooperation and Child Development, 1997/1998). Both groups were tested in three areas to determine their readiness for school. The investigators "observed (the) performance" of the children and "assessed their abilities to count, identify colours and exhibit manipulation skills. All three competencies are required for formal learning. Non-formal education imparted at anganwadis is expected to develop in the children these abilities" (National Institute of Public Cooperation and Child Development, 1997/1992: 118). Anganwadi workers were also asked to report on the preschool education aspect of their programme. "A majority of workers (reported that they) were devoting only 1-2 hours a day on preschool education activities. There was no way to judge the quality of this programme conducted during these hours" (National Institute of Public Cooperation and Child Development, 1997/1998: 116). Nevertheless, the study concluded that preschool education, not unlike the type described by Sharma in 1987, had the effect of getting children to primary school and keeping them there for longer than those children who had not attended an anganwadi. The study did not speculate on how the children acquired their abilities, for example, counting to 50, which is beyond the expectations for Standard One Class (Grade one) as set by the Government of India's Ministry of Education, nor was the study longitudinal. Parents were asked to report on the preschool experience of older siblings of ICDS children who were already enrolled in primary school.

Despite these limitations, the study has been used as evidence that the ICDS programme has achieved all of its main objectives (health, nutrition and education). Yet, in describing it success, experts decry its methods. In 1998, Sharma wrote:

'The preschool scenario in ICDS has been quite disappointing and devoid of the real emphasis on child-centred playway activities and nurturing the joy and creativity of the young child. Nevertheless, despite its poor quality, empirical evidence has indicated its positive impact on young children.' (1998: 292)

Community surveys have noted that preschool education is the most popular service of ICDS anganwadis (National Institute of Public Cooperation and Child Development, 1997-98: 58), and that parents prefer formal instruction for their children. Early on, formal preschool education was tacitly accepted by the National Institute of Public Co-operation and Child Development, the main organization responsible for training workers. The Manual on Integrating Child Development Services noted that "children invariably bring slates or takties (wooden slates for writing that are a feature of primary school)(to the anganwadis) with them. Any attempt to discontinue the element of formal learning might create problems and a credibility gap between the child and the community" (National Institute of Public Co-operation and Child Development, 1984: 55). A booklet published by United Nation's Children's Fund (no date: 24) on the ICDS used a similar argument. "Preschool education in a non-formal setting forms the backbone of the ICDS programme as all services converge on the pre-school center... The main function of the preschool education component is to stimulate and satisfy the curiosity of the child, and rather than following any rigid learning curriculum, children are taught songs and games." However, "since there is no formally structured curriculum, and flexibility is encouraged, the anganwadi often responds to parental demands to teach the alphabet and elementary numeracy". Thus, a situation evolved in which the non-formal and flexible aspects of preschool education left the way open for the introduction of academic instruction.

According to Joshi (1995), who operates preschool as part of a non-governmental organization (NGO) in the Indian Himalayas, one reason why parents prefer formal instruction in preschools is a lack of confidence in playway to prepare children for teacher-directed, test-oriented primary schools. The villagers viewed the playway method as "just song and dance"

(Joshi: 28), thus deriding the very aspect of the approach noted as the strength of anganwadis in which "children are taught songs and games" (United Nations Children's Fund, no date: 24). Joshi recommended that NGOs overcome this bias by avoiding the balwadi (kindergarten) nomenclature entirely. "Call them *hamari bal pathshala* (little schools)", so there is less resistance to the idea. All villagers preferred the term 'schools' (Joshi, 1995: 28). At the same time, Joshi, who was trained in the Montessori approach, warned against replacing playway with formal instruction.

"There is an attitude among NGOs and others that is dismissive of the use of play materials and child-centred methods as an urban, elite import, and as an indulgence that they can ill-afford in the circumstances in which they work. This attitude needs to be explored and discussed with the agencies involved. Perhaps, the hidden curriculum of authoritarian teaching methods is to demand submission to authority and it is no coincidence that we find such methods popular and prevalent in rural and working class areas. Is the privilege of learning to question authority and think independently only to be limited to our elite schools as a matter of policy?" (Joshi, 1995: 45)

Playway in Private Sector Preschools

Formal teaching in preschools, however, cuts across class lines. Just as there is no single version of playway, various methods are employed in 'preparatory' preschools—those institutions directed solely at preparing children for formal schooling. What the schools have in common is that they do not subscribe to learning through play. This does not mean that children do not play, but that the worlds of work and play are distinct in these school settings (Viruru, 1998). In the context of preparatory preschools, children's play is not children's work, as it has been portrayed in Western play theory.

Private-sector preschools in India are numbered at anywhere between 50,000 and 100,000 (Swaminathan, 1993). While some entrepreneurs operate as separate enterprises, many others are attached to private primary schools. Most preschool experts in India oppose the growth of an unregulated preschool education sector. Swaminathan (1998) wrote that in private preschools:

'Untrained teachers in ill-equipped classrooms (cram) the three Rs forcibly down the throats of unwilling children, while ignorant managements enforce inappropriate curriculum and methods of teaching, at the cost of parents who, ironically, often pay a fee they can ill afford for this dubious service, resembling torture.' (p. 22).

Some of the schools have a reputation as teaching shops that do not respect the developmental needs of their young students. Children are enrolled from the age of two-and-a-half or three, and the programme is completely oriented toward their future school success. The preschools are criticized for their role in socializing children "into the authoritarian reality of the Indian education system" (Mohite, 1998). Talking amongst children is forbidden, and there is an almost total focus on reading and writing (Department of Human Development and Family Studies, 1997). The former head of the Department of Preschool and Elementary Education at the Government of India's National Council for Educational Research and Training wrote that "almost 95 per cent of preschools in the private sector are functioning as a downward extension of the primary school" (Kaul, 1998: 67). The curriculum can include content that is beyond the official curriculum for the early primary grades. The language of instruction is most often English, which many parents consider to be necessary for success in school and career (Di Bona, 1998).

In short, preschool in India is a serious business. The extent to which this is true is evident in the growth of a sub-preschool level. Pre-nursery schools prepare children for nursery school admission tests. The overheated competition for places in the most sought after schools feeds the need for pre-primary classes which in turn, create a demand for pre-nursery school classes. Because of the special role of pre-primary classes in the schooling hierarchy (it is often the only point of entry into the most popular schools), the pre-school or pre-nursery school can have a higher fee than the primary levels. Parents correctly see preschool as a gateway to later schooling. This is true in other countries with a highly competitive secondary and higher education system. In turn, the competitive process helps to make the best private schools appear more successful. Commenting on the situation in Kenya, Sestini wrote that,

> 'Children who attend 'good' preschools are selected by the head teachers of 'good' primary schools and have increased chances of entry into 'good' secondary schools. This practice is not merely the product of parental pressure to facilitate the achievement of their children, it is also a reflection of the need for principals of schools to produce 'successful' students.' (Sestini, 1985: 29).

In fact, when compared with public schools, private schools do produce more successful students because they provide them with "the skills necessary to continue in school" (test taking skills), rather than necessarily teaching the official curriculum (Bashir, 1997: 155). In contrast, "In public schools ... the best pupils will succeed, but the majority will not acquire even rudimentary skills of literacy and numeracy" (Bashir: 155). In this climate, convincing parents of the value of child-centred playway is a formidable task.

Conclusion

In their discussion of culture and play, Roopanarine *et al.* wrote "Unfortunately, in some developing countries, the play intervention strategies imported from the post-industrialized world are adopted in a wholesale manner because of their perceived superior quality. That is, they must 'be good' because they come from the developed world" (Roopanarine *et al.*, 1998: 210). More than a half-century earlier, Gandhi (1945) offered a similar warning concerning Montessori's approach: "scientific education with Western trappings might prove poisonous to the city dwellers because here, education begins the moment the child is conceived and ends no one knows when" (370-71).

Play-based preschool education in India is the result of many influences. The idea that children learn best through play has Indian as well as Western sources. The range of preschool programmes offered by the public and private sectors in India is vast, as is evident in subsequent chapters in this volume. These include many excellent and innovative programmes largely unknown outside of their community or region. As Di Bona (1998: 274) observed, the Italian Reggio Emilia preschools are "an inspiring story, but no more so than countless examples around India that have not yet been told". Some of these stories were described in a recent book edited by Swaminathan (1998). However, as stressed throughout this chapter, programmes based on playway are rare.

The preparatory focus of pre-primary education in Indian mirrors a worldwide trend towards a more structured curricula and a focus on outcomes based education in the early years (Goffin, 1994: Wood and Bennett, 1999: Woodrow and Brennan, 1999). There is, however, opposition to this movement. In India, there are efforts to dampen the competitive nature of preschools in the private-sector through regulatory and voluntary measures. Leaders at the highest level of the early education hierarchy in universities, government and NGOs are tireless in their drive for play-based education. Efforts have also been made on the legal front. In 1997, the Delhi High Court banned interviews for admissions to pre-primary classes, although the measure had limited success ('Teething Trouble', 1997). In the state of Maharashtra (of which Mumbai is the capital), pre-primary schools must be registered under the Preschool Centres Act of 1996, an attempt to establish standards of operation and admission ('Poll Playtime', 1998). In the private sector in most states, reforms are mainly voluntary measures such as those promoted by PRAYAS (endeavour) member schools in Vadodara, Gujarat. These include the use of a lottery system for admission, the selection of children from the local community, and support for informal approaches to teaching and learning. However, the likelihood of a widespread increase in the practice of playway may be greatest in the public sector. Eighty-five per cent of Indian children do not have any preschool experience prior to starting school (United Nations

Educational, Scientific, and Cultural Organization, 2000a. Placing the focus on playway and curriculum reform in the early primary grades). The National Policy on Education (Ministry of Human Resource Development, 1986) emphasizes the need for a child-centred and activity based approach in the early primary grades as well as in pre-primary. Consistent with this policy, in public schools in the state of Gujarat, the curriculum in the first three months of the first grade must follow the principles of Tarang or joyful learning (Mohite *et al.*, 1996). Tarang is a form of indigenous non-formal education, and is meant to guard against too rapid an introduction of academic structure in kindergarten (balwadi) and the first grade. It is too early to judge the effect of this intervention, but there is considerable hope that it will have a general impact on the quality of primary schooling.

NOTES

1. The term Playway is commonly used in countries influenced by British traditions in early education to refer to play-based education. May and Carr [2(XX)] traced the origin of the term to a book by Henry Caldwell Cook (1917) entitled, The playway: an essay on educational method.
2. The step by step programme was formed to introduce child centred methods in preschools in Eastern European and former Soviet block countries. The aim was to reform preschool practices that were developed in the past to support the Soviet state.
3. The ratio was used by Myers to express in whole numbers the percentage of children worldwide who lived beyond their first birthday at the beginning of the 1990s.
4. The Integrated Child Development Service is administrated by the Department of Women and Child Development, Ministry of Human Resource Development.

REFERENCES

Bashir, S. (1997). 'The Cost Effectiveness of Public and Private Schools: Knowledge Gaps, New Research Methodologies, and an

Application in India', in C. Colclough (ed.) *Marketizing Education and Health in Developing Countries: Miracle or Mirage?*, pp. 124-64. Oxford: Clarendon Press.

Bennett, N., E. Wood and S. Rogers (1997). *Teaching Through Play: Teacher's Thinking and Classroom Practice*, Buckingham: Open University Press.

Bereiter, C. and S. Engelmann (1996). *Teaching disadvantaged children in the preschool.* Englewood Cliffs, NJ: Prentice-Hall.

Bholgle, S. (1999). 'Gender Roles: The construct in the Indian Context', in T.S. Saraswathi (ed). *Culture, Socialization and Human Development: Theory, Research, and Socialization in India.* 1999, pp. 278-3000. New Delhi: Sage.

Burman, E. (1994). *Deconstructing Developmental Psychology.* London: Routledge.

Cannella, G. (1997). *Deconstructing Early Childhood Education: Social Justice and Revolution*, New York: Peter Lang.

Cunningham, H. (1996). 'The History of Childhood', in C.P. Hwang, M.E. Lamb, and I.R. Sigle (eds.) *Images of Childhood*, pp. 27-35. Mahwah, NJ: Lawrence Erlbaum.

D. Bona, J. (1998). 'Going Back to the Educational Future: Using Indigenous Ideas to Meet Challenges of the 21th Centure', in S. Bhattacharya (ed). *The Contested Terrain: Perspectives on Education in India*, pp. 356-79. New Delhi: Orient Longman.

Department of Human Development and Family Studies (1997). 'Early childhood Care and Education: Issues and Alternatives', Seminar for School Principals of Baroda, 10th July 1997.

Department of Women and Child Development, Government of India, Ministry of Human Resource Development. (1995). *Integrated Child Development Services.* New Delhi: Author.

'Early Childhood Programmes: Setting the pace for Learning' (1997). *Education for All Bulletin*, No. 28, available online at *http://www2.unesco.org/efa/index.html* (accessed on May 17, 2000).

Elkind, D. (1988). *Miseducation: Preschoolers at Risk.* New York: Alfred A. Knopf.

Faculty of Home Science, Maharaja Sayajirao University of Baroda (1999). *'Faculty Magazine'*, Golden Jubilee Commemorative Issue. Vadodara: Author.

Ford, E. and P. Coughlin (1999). 'The Step By Step Program: Linking Democracy and Early Childhool Educatiion', *Young Children 54(4)*: 32-35.

Fox, D. and I Prilleltensky (1997). *Critical Psychology: An Introduction.* Thousand Oaks, CA: Sage.

Gakura, O.N. (1992). "Class and Pre-School Education in Kenya', unpublished Ph.D. dissertation, University of Nairobi.

Goffin, S.G. (1994). *Curriculum Models and Early Childhood Education: Appraising the Relationship.* Toronto: Maxwell Macmilan.

Greenberg, P. (1990). 'Ideas that work with young children. Why not academic preschool? Part 1', *Young Children 47(3):* 54-64.

James, A., C. Jenks and A. Prout (1998). *Theorizing Childhoold.* New York: Teachers College Press.

Jipson, J. (1991). 'Developmentally Appropriate Practice: Culture, Curriculum, Connections', *Early Education and Development* 2(2): 120-36.

Joshi, V. (1995). 'Little school on the Hill: Child Education in Community Development', *SURAKSHA: Early Childhood Care and Education in India,* Vol. 3. Chennai: M.S. Swaminathan Research Foundation.

Kaul, V. (1992). 'Early Childhood Education in India', in G. Woodill, J., Bernhard, L. and L. Prochner (eds.) *International Handbook of Early Childhood Education,* pp. 275-92. New York; Garland.

Kaul, V. (1998). 'Minimum Standards Quality in Early Childhood Education', in Report of the National Consultation Meet on Streamlining of Early Childhood Services, New Delhi, 26-17 March, 1999, pp. 57-60. New Delhi: National Institute of Public Co-operation and Child Development.

Liddel, C. and P. Kruger (1987). 'Activity and Social Behaviour in a Crowded South African Nursery: Some Effects of Crowding', *Merrill Palmer Quarterly* 33(2): 195-216.

Mani, R.S. (1961). *The Educational Ideas and Ideals of Gandhi and Tagore: A Comparative Study with Relevance to Modern India.* New Delhi: New Book Society of India.

Ministry of Human Resource Development, Department of Education, Government of India. (1986, with Modifications undertaken in 1992) 'National Policy on Education'. New Delhi: Author.

Mohite, P., H. Mankodi and J. Shastri (1996). *Tarang: The Gujarat Experience.* Report of the Proceedings of the International Seminar on School Effectiveness and Classroom Practices, National Council for Education Research and Training, New Delhi.

Muralidharan, R. and V. Kaul (1993). 'Early Childhood Care and Education: Current Status and Problems, in T.S. Saraswathi and K. Baljit (eds.) *Human Development and Family Studies in India: An Agenda for Research and Policy,* pp. 245-63. New Delhi: Sage.

Myers, R. (1992). *The Twelve Who Survive: Strengthening Programmes in Early Childhood Development in the Third World.* New York: Routledge.

National Institute of Public Co-operation and Child Development, Department of Women and Child Development, Ministry of Human Resource Development, Government of India. (1996) *National Consultation on Innovative Approaches to ICDS Training. A Report*. Bangalore, September 10-12, 1996.

National Institute of Public Co-operation and Child Development. (1997, revised reprint, or.pub. 1992) *National Evaluation of Integrated Child Development Services (India)*. New Delhi: Author.

Ogbu, J. (1981). 'Origins of Human Competence: A Cultural-Ecological Prespective', *Child Development* 52: 413-26.

Olmstead, P. and D. Weikart (1989). *How Nations Serve Young Children: Profiles of Child Care and Education in 14 Countries*. Ypsilanti, MI: High/Scope.

Poll Playtime (19 January 1998). *India Today*. Available Online At: *http://www.indiatoday.com/today/19011998/Newsnote.html* (Accessed on May 1, 2000.

Rajalakshmi, M.S. (1998). 'A Gem Among Women' in *The Children's Garden School Society, Souvenir—1937-1998*, p. 19. Chennai: Children's Garden School.

Rajalakshmi, M.S. (no date) *Under the banyan Tree*. Available From the Children's Garden School Society, Mylapore, Chennai.

Roopnarine, J.L., L. Lasker, M. Sacks and M. Stores (1988) The Cultural Contexts of Children's Play, in O.N. Saracho and B. Spodek (eds.) *Multiple Perspectives on Play in early Childhood Education*, pp. 194-219. Albany: State University of New York Press.

Roopnarine, J.L., Z. Hossain, P. gill and H. Bropgy (1994). 'Play in the East Indian Context', in J. Roopnarine, J. Johnson, and F. Hooper (eds.) *Children's Play in Diverse Cultures*. Albany: State University of New York Press.

Saracho, O.N. and B. Spodek (1998). A Historical Overview of Theories of Play, in O.N. Saracho and B. Spodek (eds.) *Multiple Perspectives on Play in early Childhood Education*, pp. 1-10. Albany: State University of New York Press.

Saraswathi, T.S., A. Verma and D. Kaira (1988). *Issues in Child Development: Curriculum, Training, Employment*. Bombay: Somaiya.

Schmetzer, U. (17 January 2000). 'India Uses Parade to Warn Pakistan', B1, B6.

Schweinhart, L.J. and D.P. Weikart (1998). 'Why Curriculum Matters in Early Childhood Education', *Educational Leadership 55 (6)*: 57 60.

Seefeldt, C. and A. Galper (1998). 'Lessons from Ukraine', *Childhood Education 74(3)*: 136-42.

Sestni, (1985). Preschool Education: Recent Devlopments in Preschool Policies and Provision in Developing Countries and the U.K., in K.. Lillis (ed.) *School and Community in Less Developed Areas*, pp. 24-41. Beckenham, UK: Croon Helm.

Sharma, A. (1987). *Monitoring Social Components of Integrated Child Development Services: A Pilot Project*. New Delhi: National Council for Educational Research and Training.

Shastri, J. (1997). *Analysis of Chetan Balwadi Curriculum.* Unpublished Report, Department of Human Development and Family Studies, Maharaja Sayajirao University of Baroda, Vadodara, India.

Shri Dakshinamurti Vidyarthi Bhavan. (no date) 'A Glimpse' (brochure). Bhanagar: Author.

Sinha, A. (1998). *Primary Schooling in India.* New Delhi: Vikas.

Stern, R.W. (1993). *Changing India: Bourgeois Revolution on the Subcontinent*. Cambridge: Cambridge University Press.

Swaminathan, M. (1993). 'Current Issues in Early Childhood Care and Education', in T.S. Saraswathi and K. Baljit (eds.) *Human Development & Family Studies in India: An Agenda for Research and Policy*, pp. 221-32. New Delhi: Sage.

Swaminathan, M. (1998). *The First Five Years: A Critical Perspective on ECCE in India.* New Delhi: Sage.

Teething Trouble (3 November 1997). *India Today.* Available online at *http://www.indiatoday.com/itoday/03111997/newsnot.html* [Accessed on February 1, 2000].

Tobin, J., D. Wu and D. Davidson (1989). *Preschool in Three Cultures: Japan, China, and the United States.* New Haven, CT: Yale University Press.

United Nations Children's Fund, (no date 'a') *ICDS in India.* New Delhi: Author.

United Nations Children's Fund. (1996). *The State of the Worlds' Children.* Oxford: Oxford University Press.

United Nations Educational, Scientific and Cultural Organisation (1996). 'Education for All, Achieving the Goal: Statistical Document', Mid-Decade Meeting fo the International Consultative forum on Education for All, 16-19 June 1996. Amman, Jordan. Paris: Author.

United Nations Educationl, Scientific and Cultural Organization. (1983). *Shareable Experiences in ECCE: A Synthesis of Case Studies.* Paris: Author.

Viruru, R. and G.S. Cannella (1997). 'An Indian Voice in the Education of Young Children', *International Journal of Educational Reform* 6(3): 308-15.

Wood, E. and N. Bennet (1999). 'Progression and Continuity in Early Childhood Education: Tensions and Contractions', *International Journal of Early Education 7(1)*: 5-16.

Woodhead, M. (1996). *In Search of the Rainbow: Pathways to Quality in Large-Scale Programmes for Young Disadvantaged Children.* Early Childhood: Practice and Reflections, Vol. 10. The Hague: Bernard van Ler Foundation.

Woodill, G., J. Bernhard and L. Prochner (1992). *International Handbook of Early Childhood Education*, New York: Garland.

Woodrow, C. and M. Brennan (1999). 'Marketised Positioning of Early Childhood: New Contexts for Curriculum and Professional Development in Queensland, Australia', *Contemporary Issues in Early Childhood 1991*: 78-94.

3

The Project Approach in an Indian Context

LILIAN KATZ, PRERANA MOHITE and JIGISHA SHASTRI

THE PROJECT APPROACH: AN INDIAN EXPERIENCE

I. The Project Approach

The inclusion of investigation projects in the curriculum for young children was first reported early in the last century as applied at University of Chicago Laboratory School. Shortly thereafter, this approach was promoted as a method of teaching in elementary schools by William Heard Kilpatrick (1922) under the title "The Project Method". The project method also became a major component of British infant and primary education following World War II and up until the 1980s. It can also be seen as a component of the world-renowned pre-primary schools of the small northern Italian city of Reggio Emilia (Katz, 1997). The experience of the pre-primary educators in Reggio Emilia has deepened our understanding of how what they call the 'graphic languages', can enrich the development and learning of very young children, and can do so much earlier than had been previously believed. The rich experience in Reggio Emilia has also deepened our understanding of the value of incorporating the careful use of documentation of the children's experiences to enhance all aspects of children's learning and the experiences of their parents as well.

The project approach recommended today by Katz and Chard (1989), and Helm and Katz (2001) and discussed and illustrated in this chapter is more carefully structured than earlier implementations.

We define a project as an in-depth investigation of a particular topic, usually undertaken by a whole class, in which sub-groups focus on sub-topics related to the main one. The term Project Approach is used to suggest that the projects constitute an important element of an early childhood curriculum. When well implemented, the Project Approach complements other aspects of the curriculum. For example, in project work, academic skills are used purposefully in the service of children's intellectual pursuits, and their recommended: inclination to use the basic skills are strengthened by the obvious usefulness of those skills in the eyes of children themselves.

The central feature of project work is that it involves children in conducting their own research. On the basis of discussions with their teachers, the children formulate a set of questions about the phenomenon under investigation (e.g., the local supermarket), and with the teacher, plan how to gather information, and how to represent their findings.

The Phases of Project Work

The investigation of a project is usually divided into three phases. This, process helps young children gain a sense of the experiences included in conducting the investigation. By conducting their work in the three phases, children can identify readily with the purpose of the work of each phase and enjoy a sense of the progression of their efforts.

Phase I—Getting Started

In phase I, a topic is selected, usually by the teacher through discussions with the children on the basis of which, she can assess the likelihood that the topic will interest a large proportion of the children in the class. During these early discussions, the children share with others their experiences and current knowledge related to the topic, and conclude with a set of research questions to be answered by the investigation. During phase I, the children are also encouraged to represent their own experiences related to the topic through drawing, painting, dictating stories, reporting their memories and sharing what they already know about the topic with their classmates. The teacher is able to assess what aspects of the topic are likely to be of greatest interest and are in need of greatest clarification through the investigations undertaken by the children. As seen in the description that follows of the three year olds' exploration of a dog, the teachers could easily see how the children understood and misunderstood the purpose and uses of the dog's collar as they likened it to a belt, normally used to hold up trousers!

At the close of Phase I, the teacher helps the children, formulate their research questions and predict what the answers to those questions are likely to be. The teacher also provokes the children into explaining the bases of their predictions. The children are encouraged to predict the answers to their questions (e.g. How many different kinds of cereal will be at the supermarket and which kind is sold most?) and to share the bases for their predictions. This phase may last several days, or a week or two, depending on how often the children are together, and their interest in the topic.

Phase II—Gathering the Data

During this period, the main activity is conducting the investigation and doing the fieldwork involved in gathering data that will answer the questions they formed during Phase I. Phase II also includes planning how to represent their actual findings. Depending on the ages of the children and the nature of the topic, Phase II will include first-hand, direct exploration of the objects and environments related to the topic. The visits to various relevant places include children drawing what they are observing, asking questions to the on-site experts, as well as inviting experts to their classroom to show them relevant items and answer their questions. Many projects also include the children conducting surveys related to the topic and interviewing people who have something to say about the topic, as can be seen in the description that follows of the children's visit to a garage. Towards the end of this phase the children discuss with the teacher what representations they will create, drawing and charts to be mounted, and other ways of presenting the results of their research.

Phase III—Bringing the Investigation to a Conclusion

During this final period, the work of the investigation is brought to a close, the debriefing mainly concerning what has been learned and accomplished and presenting findings to others, such as other classes, parents, and community members. Most projects also produce displays, class books and photo albums that capture and document the children's experiences, so that they themselves can re-visit them and share them with others, who were not part of the actual experiences.

II. The Project Approach and Children's Development and Learning

Observing young children engaged in good project work makes it very clear that every aspect of development and learning can be supported by the activities and processes involved.

The teacher is also educating children's interests by introducing a topic worthy of the children's energy and effort. As the teacher engages the children in discussions related to the topic, children gain ample experience to express their views, listen to others' views, argue, explain and enhance many other verbal processes that develop during the preschool period.

In most of the work involved in conducting an investigation, children are active rather than passive learners, working in contexts which purposefully employ their emerging academic skills and their intellectual dispositions to theorize, analyze, hypothesize, make predictions and argue. The children readily take initiative and responsibility for seeking answers to their questions through a variety of information-seeking strategies, e.g. conducting interviews, surveys, observational drawing and sketching, discussions and arguments. This 'active' *versus* 'passive' role in the classroom is thought to be especially important in the development and learning of boys, who are expected to be more assertive and active rather than passive as compared to girls.

When the teacher consults the children about what aspects of their work they want to display, discuss and report to others, she provokes their growing capacities to imagine in advance how others might react to what they have to say. In other words, the purpose of these investigations and the usefulness of basic literacy and numeracy and other skills are clear to the children themselves.

In the modern Project Approach, teaching is seen not just as "covering" a subject, but helping children to "uncover" it in-depth by their investigations. Project work does not constitute the whole curriculum; rather, it is intended to complement other aspects of the curriculum in which, children are encouraged to begin mastery of basic academic skills. Furthermore, extensive experience of involving young children in good project work indicates that their capacities to persist, to overcome obstacles and set backs in the course of their work become stronger.

Another contribution of the Project Approach is that it involves children in an extended effort over time, rather than brief one-shot amusing activities. In this way, the disposition called interest, i.e. the capacity to lose oneself in something outside of oneself, can be developed and supported, and thereby strengthened. Furthermore, the use of multiple methods of documenting children's experiences during and following these investigations encourages children to revisit their experiences *via* the documentation.

As already indicated, in contrast to both, formal teacher-directed curriculum models and many "developmentally appropriate" approaches, the Project Approach emphasizes providing contexts that strengthen and support children's intellectual dispositions. This is in contrast to the formal instruction contexts that can damage these important dispositions by excessive academic pressure or by neglecting them in favour of spontaneous play and arts and crafts. The damaged-disposition hypothesis seems a reasonable interpretation of the results of several longitudinal comparative studies of curriculum approaches (See Golbeck, 2001; Marcon, 2002). As we look at the results of these studies, the early pressure on young children to perform academic tasks taught by direct instruction (e.g., practice in phonics, repetition, reciting in unison, workbook exercises) appears not only harmless, but also beneficial at first. Certainly, many of the children can and do perform the tasks on which they have been drilled.

However, on the whole, these studies suggest that while formal instruction during the preschool years appears beneficial in the short-term, it shows negative effects on the academic, intellectual, and social developments in the long-term. Results from these longitudinal studies support the view that curriculum design for young children should be approached in a way that optimizes simultaneously the acquisitions of knowledge, skills and desirable dispositions, which in turn can strengthen their motivation to master a variety of skills and to persist at challenging tasks (Dweck, 1999). It is clearly not very useful to have acquired skills if the dispositions to use them are undermined in the process of their acquisition. On the other hand, having the disposition for example, to be a reader, without having the necessary skills is also inconsistent with the goals of education. The challenge then, is to help learners with both, the acquisition of skills and with the dispositions that invoke the application of those skills. The modern Project Approach provides ample opportunity for such simultaneous learning to occur.

The Indian Preschools: A brief Overview

The paper presents a brief overview of The Project Approach as tried out in the Laboratory Nursery School, Chetan Balwadi, of the Department of Human Development and Family Studies, Faculty of Home Science, The Maharaja Sayajirao University of Baroda, Vadodara.

The Laboratory School has three classes; younger group, older group and kindergarten. Children in these classes are 3, 4, and 5 years of age respectively. Each class has a programme framework which has its base in the relevant developmental level of children. The framework guides in planning weekly programmes. A thematic approach is followed, with one topic chosen for a week or two. The environment is organized based on the theme. Bulletin boards have related topics and mobiles are hung in the environment. The doll house in the class often gets converted into a shop, hospital or library, depending on the theme of the week. Children are provided opportunities for first hand experiences and are encouraged to conduct experiments on their own.

The Project Approach as a systematic venture began in 1997. Prof. Lillian Katz was a visiting Professor to the Department of Human Development and Family Studies, Faculty of Home Science, The Maharaja Sayajirao University of Baroda, Vadodara. Under her guidance and with her direct involvement, the faculty began the project on 'Books' in the kindergarten class. Then on, the project approach became a regular feature of the programme and various themes have been selected over the years in all the three classes i.e. Younger Group, Older Group and the Kindergarten.

Following is a description of two select projects, one each from younger group and Kindergarten Classes.

Animals

On a field trip the younger children (3 years of age) encountered goats on the road. The children were fascinated with them. They touched, observed and talked to them. An interest arose to know more about animals and thus the project on animals began. Thus, a related experience presents in the children's environment served as a source for selection of the topic (Mohite, Mankodi, Shastri, Jasrai, 1997).

During the first phase of the project, the teachers initiated discussion on animals. Children's responses were noted. The classroom environment was geared to the topic of animals. Pictures on bulletin boards, mobiles, photographs and models were arranged for the children to observe and explore. Then began the 2nd phase of fieldwork. Children made varied field trips in small groups. They visited a mini zoo of a nearby school and the city zoo in Kamatibaug. A baby goat, a dog and a rabbit were brought to the class.

The actual experience of first hand exploration of the animals was very rewarding. The little dog invoked responses like:

1st child—It's white in colour and has long ears.
2nd child—It has a belt on its neck.
3rd child—Because it might run away otherwise.
2nd child—But belt is to be worn with a pant.
3rd child—We wear a tie on neck and not a belt.
4th child—It has hair on it's body.
1st child—They are soft.

This led to an understanding about the animal, its body parts, characteristics and habits. At the same time, additional concepts were learnt and differences and similarities between accessories used by children and the animals emerged. (e.g. belt *vs.* tie).

In the next stage, a zoo was created. Children used bricks for a boundary wall and mud for the floor. With the teacher's suggestion fenugreek seeds were sown. The little green shoots looked like green grass. Animal pictures pasted on a stick were put in various places. Cages for the animals were built with twigs. Tiny ceramic pots were put as water bowls. During this whole process, there was active discussion going on among the children. Ideas came forth, pros and cons were discussed. Some ideas were retained and few were dismissed. Everyday, children sat near the zoo and "talked to" these "animals". They would lead the "stick animal" to the ceramic pot "to drink water". Thus, dramatization took place. The children expressed concern about care of their animals at night, in their absence.

Even after the project was discontinued, the zoo became a corner in the classroom for action, discussion and conversation.

Main Features: Conversation, Dramatization, Actual Exploration of Animals

Vehicles

It is generally found that vehicle is a topic of interest for kindergarten children. Everyday a majority of them commute in a rickshaw (a three wheeler) and as soon as they enter the class, the discussion is about which other vehicles they overtook on the road, other vehicles they saw, etc. Hence, vehicle as a theme was selected (Shastri & Bhagia, 1997).

The project began with a general discussion on the topic. It was found that in the initial stage, children learnt new names of various vehicles like cycle, scooter, scooty, luna, kinetic, sunny, etc. Their discussion centred around vehicles they possessed. They were very curious to know which vehicles their friends had and its specifics like the colour, make etc.

The doll house had tools and toy vehicles. Boys especially dramatized roles of a repair man, petrol pump service man, driver on the road, ticket collector and passengers. "Paper Money" was exchanged for work done.

Pictures on the bulletin board and books in the language corner were looked at and read.

Children were curious to know how many and what kinds of vehicles were seen on the road. The class was divided into two groups. Each group selected a different road side to stand and observe the vehicles passing by and they carried with them papers with pictures of vehicles pasted on it. A few children observed the vehicles and others tally marked their frequency. Thus, children had an opportunity for practicing counting skills and processes of classification and discrimination were reinforced.

Dramatization in the sand play also reflected the theme of vehicles. Sand was used to build a train with an engine and carriages. There were "connecting chains" with sticks between carriages. Accessories like sticks, buttons, metal pieces were used to make the light, chimney and other parts of the engine.

Children went to the parking area for fieldwork. A specific visit was arranged at a car garage–service station–Cargo Motors.

Play in the doll house and outdoors reflected change in the vocabulary and use of new "equipment". They made vehicles with clay, depicting details with accessories. Chalk drawings on the floor too reflected their understanding and interest in different vehicles and its specific details.

At the end of two weeks, their interest declined and hence the project was brought to an end.

Main Features: Conversation, Counting, Classification, Discrimination, Representation

Children's Learning: Process and Concepts

During initiation and implementation of these projects, a wide range of learning took place in children.

It is clearly evident from examples of Projects documented earlier that development took place in all the areas, namely language, communication, social, emotional, and cognitive development. Children learnt new concepts, clarified misconceptions, learnt new vocabulary, developed skills of conversation and learnt to count and read.

One of the areas in which development was evident was language. Children gained new vocabulary be it related to vehicles, say for e.g. words like diesel and petrol, jack and spanner. The youngest group learnt names of different animals and the food they ate.

Children sat in small groups and planned questions they wanted to ask at the garage. They planned who will ask which question. When they reached the garage, the planned questions were forgotten but new questions emerged. The men working in the garage were very enthused at the children's questioning.

"How much money do you charge?"

"When do you service the cars?"

"How do you fix the rear lights?"

The children had gone to the garage with their drawing boards. In the beginning, they went about in a group observing everything. Then they sat down to represent their observations. The drawings depicted the cars involved in accidents which had been brought for repair, a huge lift that could carry a car, cars viewed from different angles, car jack, car being painted etc.

The next day, the discussion focused on the visit to the garage. They remembered the names of different cars, specific the actions of the work men, parts of the cars and the machinery. The visit to the garage led to an increase in vocabulary related to vehicles and related mechanical equipment. Identification of the equipment, its purpose, process involved in repairing and cleaning of vehicles was recalled by children in a sequence.

Chetan Balwadi being a Laboratory preschool, active interaction was always encouraged in children. However, a significant change in the mode of interaction was observed through the implementation of the Project Approach. Earlier, the group sessions involved conversation between the teacher and children. Though children actively participated, their questions as well as answers were directed to the teachers. With the Project Approach, there was an effort of directing the questions to each other. They argued, hypothesized, discussed and came to conclusions.

The children also learnt questioning as a skill, especially questioning strangers. They discovered it as an active way to gather information.

Another distinct difference was that most of their conversations through the day were now directed towards the topic being studied. Interest in the topic was sustained for a longer period of time.

For the older children, interest and involvement in reading and writing increased. As the Laboratory school's programme is individualized and developmentally appropriate, children have never been pressurized into reading and writing. Reading and writing have always been with reference to ongoing themes/projects. Through the Project Approach children started documenting what they observed.

This helped them in communicating to each other their experiences. Their own drawings helped them remember details which they otherwise forgot. They also realized the importance of documentation. They realized that documenting experiences helped in better communication. They could share with each other what they had seen. It triggered off their memory and they remembered more details. Children who were hesitant earlier started experimenting with alphabets.

Math too become a natural daily life activity. Counting and measuring were everyday activities. This enhanced their numerical concepts. They learnt seriation, size, shape, volume, and measurement.

Thus, the Project Approach encouraged children to be more 'active participants' in the learning process.

At the same time, some constraints were experienced. In the Indian context, children are not used to asking too many questions. In fact, in the Indian culture, children are not expected or encouraged to ask questions. Hence, questioning by children seemed at times contrived and most of the times, they either forgot their questions or forgot to ask the questions.

The other issue is that of teacher-child interaction. Adults are considered authority figures and are supposed to know more than children. Therefore, rather than discussing things with each other and contradicting each other, children sought the teacher's opinions. This is very natural in an Indian situation. Infact, children would be satisfied with an answer only if and when it was confirmed by the teacher.

The third is a practical problem of resources. Schools lack both, adequate human as well as financial resources necessary for field trips and may not necessarily have vehicles for travel. Sometimes, even the art material is limited and cannot be used by children at their own free will.

Any strategy has to be weighed in the cultural context to which the children belong. The Project Approach that has evolved in the Indian setting includes some key features of the Project Approach as conceived by Katz and Chard. Activities such as representational drawing, mirror activity, developing webs from children's responses have now become part of the programme. Representational drawing enhances children's observation skills and representational abilities.

Developing webs of children's responses provides concrete evidence of the progress of the children through the project weeks/days. The effort continues with varied themes and different groups of children.

REFERENCES

Dweck, Carol S. (1999). Caution-Praise can be dangerous, *American Educator* (23), 1, 4-9.

Golbeck, Susan L. (2001). (Ed.) *Psychological Perspectives on Early Childhood Education: Reframing Dilemmas in Research and Practice,* New Jersey: Lawrence Erlbaum Associates.

Helm, Judith H. & Katz, Lilian G. (2001). *Young Investigators: The Project Approach with Young Children,* NY: Teachers College Press.

Katz, L. & Chard, S. (1989). *Engaging children's minds: The project approach.* Norwood, NJ: Ablex.

Katz, Lilian G. (1997). The Challenges of the Reggio Emilia Approach. In Joanne Hendricks (Ed.). *First Steps Toward Teaching the Reggio Way.* Upper Saddle River: New Jersey. Merrill Prentice Hall.

Kilpatrick, W.H. (1922). The Project Method. *Teachers College Record.* 19(4). 319-35.

Marcon, Rebecca (2002). Moving up the Grades: Relationship Between Preschool Model and Later School Success. *Early Childhood Research and Practice. <http://ecrp.uiuc.edu/v4/n1/marcon.html>.*

Mohite, P., Mankodi, H., Shastri, J., Jasrai, S. (1997). *The project approach: An Indian experience.* Unpublished project report. Chetan Balwadi: The laboratory nursery school, Department of Human Development and Family Studies, Faculty of Home Science, The Maharaja Sayajirao University of Baroda, Vadodara.

Shastri, J. & Bhagia, D. (1997). *Broom broom...peep peep pipip peep...zoo...oom: Project vehicles,* Unpublished Project report. Chetan Balwadi: The Laboratory Nursery School, Department of Human Development and Family Studies, Faculty of Home Science, The Maharaja Sayajirao University of Baroda, Vadodara.

4

Play and Young Children with Special Needs

NEERJA SHARMA

The discussion in this chapter is being presented in the following seven sections:

1. The rationale
2. Disability and the need to play
3. Cultural-familial construction of play and disability
4. Early childhood special education in India
5. Antecedents of play in children
6. 'Teaching' children to play for development, learning and self-esteem
7. Conclusion

The examples of children's play in the text are extracted from actual observations made at current education programmes. While the names of the student-trainees are real and mentioned with their permission, those of the children and teachers are changed to protect their identity.

The Rationale

One may ask—why do we need a separate discussion on play for children with special needs?—an expression operationally used here for those with disabilities. There must be a convincing rationale to do so in a volume devoted to play and early childhood education in India. There are several reasons—demographic, cultural, developmental and educational. Demographic data informs us that there are an enormous number of young children with disabilities in India. They need care-giving of a more sensitive kind than ordinarily available to a child, and play is a valuable component in this care.

Culturally speaking, Indian families are generally intense on affect in their socialization of children, and are person-focused rather than activity-oriented in their caregiving of the child. Sometimes, that precludes deliberate attempts of play with the child—a practice that may not be in the larger interest of the child with disability.

Developmental needs of children with disability are similar to those of normally growing children. However, their development itself may be delayed or disturbed by disabling conditions—congenital or environmental. Depending upon the nature of the child's impairment, developmental milestones are achieved late. Since play behaviour matches stages in cognitive development (Piaget, 1962) a delay in acquiring cognitive skills, that accompanies most types of childhood disabilities, implies retardation in exploratory and play skills. Stimulation of play behaviour in children has been recognized as an intervention strategy in conditions of deprivation (Anandalakshmy, 1990; Sharma, 1989). This argument can be extended, and will be supported with evidence in this chapter, to reiterate that not only is play necessary for development, it is a valuable tool in enhancing cognitive, language and social-emotional development. Above all, the child has a right to play for its own sake, as enshrined in Article 31 of the Convention of the Rights of the Child, 1990 (ICCW, 1994).

The educational justification in emphasizing play for children with disabilities is self evident. The argument is not any more for why, but how to incorporate play activities in children's learning and development in early childhood education programmes. Sensitive and well-trained educators can make children's entry and stay in a preschool wholly enjoyable through their use of play and game-based approach to learning activities.

Play is a voluntary activity, but all voluntary activities are not play. Thus, if a child with autism caresses his ball repetitively, it is not play, as play is said to include those activities of the child that are spontaneous as well as self-generating (Lowenfeld, 1935). In my experience with children in educational settings, when they have intellectual, locomotor or sensory disabilities, spontaneous play is not common. When not being guided, they may show movement, restlessness or repetitive action, but play behaviour is generally not present.

If present, it is in its rudimentary and regressive forms. This is not to say that the children do not or cannot enjoy play; rather, they need to be helped to experience the fun and joy of playing with peers, adults and toys for them to want it again.

Disability and the Need to Play

At this point, it seems appropriate to define who are the children we refer to as having special needs. There are medical, psychological and educational taxonomies of childhood disabilities. In this chapter, we will adopt a classification that seems most fair to children who are likely to be in early childhood education settings:

(i) *Children with Intellectual Impairments*: This expression is being used here to replace the term mental retardation. The word "mental" has connotations other than cognitive, while the term "intellectual" has specific reference to intelligence related abilities. The word "impairment" denotes a state of damage to the person, freeing the child of the label of "containing retardation" or "being retarded". Thus, it may be possible that in certain contexts, the child with intellectual impairment is not regarded as retarded or handicapped; he/she is not compared with others for competencies and is accepted for whatever he/she can do.

Nevertheless, the most acceptable definition of intellectual impairment comes from the American Association on Mental Retardation that it revised in

1992. It reads as follows: "Mental retardation refers to substantial limitations in present functioning. It is characterized by significantly sub-average intellectual functioning, existing concurrently with related limitations in two or more of the following applicable adaptive skill areas: communication, self-care, home living, social skills, community use, self-direction, health and safety, functional academics, leisure and work. Mental retardation manifests before age 18 (Smith & Luckasson, 1995: 136).

(ii) *Children with Health Impairments and Physical Disabilities*: This category includes children with health problems that limit the body's physical well-being and require on-going medical attention. It also includes children who have limitations due to the structure or functioning of the body caused by defects in limbs, bones, joints or muscles. Some examples are juvenile diabetes, spina bifida, and cerebral palsy.

(iii) *Children with Visual Impairments*: These are children with low vision or those who cannot see at all, i.e. they are blind.

(iv) *Children with Hearing Impairments*: Like vision, hearing loss can also be partial or complete. Thus there are children who are hard of hearing and those who have no hearing, i.e., they are deaf.

(v) *Children with Language or Speech Impairments*: In this section are subsumed two categories of children. The first includes those who show delayed or deviant development of comprehension and/or expression of spoken, written or other forms of communication. The second describes those who have difficulty in the production of spoken language.

(vi) *Children with Behavioural and Emotional Disturbance*: This category has children who show behaviours and emotions unacceptable to the social group they belong to and are maladaptive for their own development and learning. For example, children showing aggressive behaviour or withdrawal symptoms.

Children's play behaviours have been observed and analyzed by pioneering researchers such as Hutt (1976) and Gravey (1977) to demonstrate that it is a window to the child's construction of reality. While a detailed discussion on how children's play achieves this can be found in another chapter of this volume, a brief mention of the significance of play in child's development is being made below for recapitulation. The idea is to stress the point that play holds the same value for children who have disabilities or disturbance.

- *Physical and Motor Function*: Through play, children demonstrate and achieve gross and fine motor control. Skills of manipulating objects, jumping and hopping are practiced during young children's play. Active movements during play strengthen children's joints and muscles.
- *Cognitive Function*: Children use play to find solutions to problems. In doing so, they study cause and effect relationships and develop organizing abilities. During play, children engage in creative thinking and experiment with new ideas.
- *Social Function*: Interactive play situations develop in children the ability to take the point of view of others, to delay gratification and to learn and express pro-social behaviours.
- *Emotional Function*: Play is the medium through which children express their needs and feelings. Acting out or role playing takes place through socio-dramatic play. Play therapy is known to be a useful method of treating children with emotional disturbance.

Since the urge to play is natural in childhood, it would be quite in order to say that children with disabilities also experience it. However, the fact that they are often not found to be engaged in spontaneous play, even when no restrictions are placed on them, points to the fact that their impairments and difficulties delimit some of their natural behaviours. For example, difficulty in or lack of mobility restricts the child's play being non-locomotive. Intellectual limitation seems to impair the ability for novel and creative forms of play. Children with visual impairment are not able to explore their environment and materials without active adult initiative, as sight is important for this to happen naturally. Their attempts are thwarted by accidents if the physical space is not made safe for them. Hearing impairment would usually pose difficulty in a child's interaction with hearing peers who use speech for communication during play. Children who are emotionally disturbed do not engage in socially desirable forms of play, and if they play, as they may be anxious, fearful, overexcited or depressed.

While specific disabilities may hinder children in specific ways during play, all children do not show low levels of motivation to play. However, the light heartedness and facetiousness often associated with play, is rarely observed among children with severe forms of disability. It is an area that needs to be researched, especially in the light of advocacy for inclusive education which can provide varying forms of interaction among disabled and non-disabled children.

In a recently concluded study of children's perception of their own disability when they attended schools for integrated education, Joshi (2001) reported that the children (5-13 years) enjoyed playing with their friends, both disabled and non-disabled. The play activities that they mentioned were—ball game, badminton, cricket, skipping, swinging or simply talking or watching others play (p. 208). Apparently, these children were not new in their schools and were able to express their likes and dislikes to the researcher.

When young children with disabilities are fresh in a programme of early childhood education, they are intrepid and do not display voluntary play behaviour. That they are new to the relatively structured situation could be one reason. However, accounts of the lives of children with disabilities reveal that their routines are crowded with activities of physical care, medical treatment and therapies (Joshi, 2001; Navalkar, 2001; Pal, 1991; Phoolka, 1990). The caregivers do not have time or the affective disposition to play with the children. The young child with a disability does not have the natural propensity to play as other children do, such as playing with household objects or engaging others to play with. Members of family often become overprotective (or sometimes neglectful) and do not foster autonomy in the child, seeing it as risky in care and treatment. Hence, not only does the child have to be taught to play, the caregivers too may require guidance on why, what and how to play with a child who has a disability.

Cultural-Familial Construction of Play and Disability

Play

The meaning of psychological phenomena that are part of human experience are culturally constructed (Chaudhary, 1999). What play and disability mean for the child is largely influenced by what the caregivers believe about them and how these are mirrored to the child during interactions. Vygotsky (1981) has emphasized the significance of social phenomena in human behaviour. Reiterating this hypothesis through her findings, Chaudhary (1999) reported significant adult mediation in the infant subjects' experience of communication, affect and play, which according to her, contextualized these experiences for the child.

Fleer (1996) has questioned the universality of predetermined developmental path in play advocated by Parten (1932) and Piaget (1962). She calls for a scrutiny of the broader cultural context in the study of how children play, as "play themes originate from the child's culture" (p. 14). She believes that "play activities of children—regardless of their type are culturally defined, valued and interpreted. They exist as a result of cultural practices" (p. 16). In his book Magical Child, Pearce (1977) is of the view that play has an epigenetic quality; like imagination and imitation, it is genetically provided for by nature. Pointing to connection between fantasy play in a social context and unfolding of creativity in childhood, he gives the example of the African Pygmy child who "plays at adult reality throughout childhood, and the adults delightedly play with the child in his learning" (p. 171).

Indian families are person-oriented in their interactions with children, including in their play. In Chaudhary's study (1999) of 25 families wherein family interaction patterns and language development in infants (6-8 months) was examined, the mothers spoke with their infants about people as contrasted with objects and events. It was also found that play with people was a more common experience as compared to play with objects. Even when toys were used, the interactions were mediated closely by the adults and references to persons were incorporated.

Patterns of play were studied among slightly older children (2-4 years) by Mehra (1995) who reported that people in the child's environment were a frequent source of play; and even in play with objects adult mediation occurred frequently. She observed that the infants were a part of the adult social world, and were constantly included in the activities of those around them. Of the 60 observations made by her at the homes of children, in 28 of them, a non-family member was present. The children had opportunities to observe adults in their daily work and imitated them in their play.

The implications of these two studies can be extended to state that being with significant others is an important part of the socialization of the Indian child, hence the play experience of the child with special needs is also likely to be person-focused rather than object/toy-oriented. Moreover, the family is likely to prioritize 'care' for the child, over and above providing play activities and materials.

Disability

The concept of disability has several meanings in India depending upon where it is situated and where it is talked about. The scenario could be many: urban, semi-urban and rural; an educated home or a barely literate or a non-literate home; a school, a hospital or a rehabilitation centre; a social context or a political one; a family or an institution and so on. The components that are believed to lend complexity to the Indian society, also contribute to the social construction of the notion of disability. Research indicates that cultural beliefs about disability play a significant role in determining the way in which families perceive disability and the steps they take for its prevention, treatment and rehabilitation (Chaturvedi & Malhotra, 1984; Sen, 1988).

Speaking of the history of views on disability in India, in the second half of the 20th century, it is the medical perspective of disability that dominated thinking among practitioners. According to this approach, the individual is disabled and handicapped by the impairments he is born with or that develop later. This view was reinforced by the medical model of the World Health Organization whose definitions of impairment, disability and handicap (Pandey & Advani, 1996) situate the problem within the individual such that the condition limits his/her participation in regular life. Thus not being able to perform "normal" activities due to physical, sensory or intellectual deficits has been regarded as disabling and handicapping for the individual. The medical framework has ignored the social and ecological barriers to normalization of disabled persons' lives.

The medical view may have gained ascendance over any other partly because the only professional helper a disabled person visits with some regularity is a medical practitioner or a paramedico for treatment. Involvement of other rehabilitation workers in work for the disabled is a recent development and still quite inadequate (Kundu, 2000).

One redeeming feature of inadequate medical and educational services, particularly in rural areas, has been non-categorization of disabled children into 'neat' sets of conditions usually made available to families that live in an informed set set-up. While children with disabilities have always been part of society, families generally have not adopted the medical or educational labels to refer to the children. Depending upon the family's own belief system or that of the community, the child is seen to suffer from a debilitating condition, to reverse which, the caregivers place faith not only in doctors, but also in traditional healers and alternate systems of medicine.

A single factor is often not seen to be the cause of disability in the child. Even when provided with medical etiology, most parents express a strong belief in the metaphysical causation (Dalal & Pandey, 1999). They invoke their belief in fate and attribute the disability to their own *karma* or that of the child (Phoolka, 1990; Pal, 1991). According to the *karma* theory as stated in Hindu philosophy, all good or bad deeds accumulate over previous births and the present suffering is explained as a consequence of the misdeeds of previous births (Dalal & Pandey, 1999). Inappropriate medical practices and treatment, and family history too are implicated by parents to explain disability in their child (Navalkar, 2001; Phoolka, 1990).

Spirituality and religion are integral to cultural perceptions about disability in India. Their role begins early as part of child's socialization in the form of sermons quoted from religious texts that enunciate a moral and spiritual code of conduct towards the weak and the disabled. The virtues that are extolled are tolerance, love and charity. Studies of Indian parents from different social class groups reveal that they cope with and strive to accept the child's disability largely through their belief in god in different ways. Some explain it as a "manifestation of divine wrath due to past *karma* of the child and the family" (Phoolka, 1990: 35), while others explain it as "God's way of making us come close to Him" (Pal, 1991: 47). Irrespective of educational levels, families hope for miraculous healing of the child and visit faith healers, shrines and temples. They may also perform religious ceremonies at home (such as *Havan*) to bring 'cure' to the child (Phoolka, 1990).

The Indian way of life permits families to visit practitioners of alternative and indigenous medicines, thus treatments through homeopathy, Unani, Ayurveda and Reiki are sought by families for the disabled child (Joshi, 2001; Navalkar, 2001). Advice and recommendations by priests, sages and shamans are also heeded with seriousness. Many parents claim an improvement in the child's development and performance, although there is no scientific study of such phenomena. A closely related and significant ecological variable that is linked with childhood disability in India is poverty. In a country of more than one billion population, there are more than 150 million children in the age range 0-6 (Registrar General of India,

2001). A very large number among these are born in economically poor circumstances, both rural and urban. They are at risk before birth and many are affected by preventable forms of disability after birth on account of the poor quality of living. Low levels of parental education and awareness, combined with inadequate resources in the community remain the unmitigated antecedents of childhood disability among the poor.

Two recent studies which are descriptive and analytic of parental response to their children's disabilities are significant in this context. Joshi (2001) has studied 49 families while researching the meaning of disability from the perspectives of children (5-13 years), their mothers and teachers. The second study is by Navalkar (2001) in which she recorded the perceptions of 13 fathers about their own role when they had a child with cerebral palsy. The findings of the two studies convey the following themes very vividly about families—there is utmost concern for and attachment with the child. Frustrations show up as bringing up the 'different' child is tough. The medical, educational and rehabilitative facilities are difficult to access, social attitudes are unsympathetic and infrastructure for care is non-supportive. However, the families continue to struggle to negotiate for the child's present and future. They do not perceive the severity of the child's disability as a variable. They discern several competencies in their child just like normal children. In Joshi's sample she found that a significant number of families (43%) had reframed their perspectives to be positive. They had developed a sense of control and competence, had redefined the child with disability for themselves and had revised the meaning of life and self such that they could experience enablement in coping with everyday life.

Early Childhood Special Education in India

The Government of India does not have a separate policy for the education and care of children with disability under six. They are addressed in policies and programmes for all children under 18. This section of the chapter deals with the issues of need for special provisions, major laws and policies, manpower development initiatives and types of services available for young children with special needs in the country.

The Need

The education of a child identified to have a developmental delay or disability must begin primarily in the form of early intervention during infancy or latest at the preschool stage. For most children, support and training are required even for simple developmental tasks such as walking, toileting, socializing and learning to speak. Intervention can be provided at a centre or at the child's home. The number of children who require such a service in India is staggering, and thus far, the proportion of young children who may be in any organized service, government or non-government, is negligible. A quick look at the demographic status of childhood disability in India would help in understanding the enormity of the problem and in stating the case for early childhood special education. The source for most of the data in this chapter is a volume titled Status of Disability in India-2000, published by the Rehabilitation Council of India (RCI) (Kundu, 2000).

The RCI is a statutory body established by the Government of India in June 1993 and is under the Ministry of Social Justice and Empowerment. It regulates the functioning of various categories of professionals working with people with disabilities, its primary function being manpower development of professionals who are engaged in the rehabilitation of persons with disabilities, to help them meet their needs throughout the life cycle. The professionals could belong to the fields of:

- Physical-medical rehabilitation,
- Educational rehabilitation,
- Vocational rehabilitation, and
- Social rehabilitation.

A UNICEF estimate has placed the figure of 30 million children out of 300 million children in the age range 0-14 years as having one or more disabilities. Another reliable source quoted by RCI is the National Sample Survey Organization (NSSO) Report, according to which the number of children with disabilities in the age group 5-14 years in 1991 were:

Locomotor handicaps	8.94 million
Hearing handicaps	3.24 million
Speech handicaps	1.96 million
Visual handicaps	4.01 million
Mental handicaps	9.00 million
Cerebral palsy	3.00 million

Thus, approximately, 10 per cent of the child population have special educational needs arising from physical or intellectual impairments. A generous estimate of RCI indicates that not more than 3-4 per cent of the children with special needs have access to education with or without support services. This number does not generally include young children below school age, i.e. under 5 years. At the time this paper was in preparation, a draft National Policy on Education for Children with Disabilities, prepared by RCI, was under discussion at the Government level and it has recommended that preschool education should be included in the policy (NIPCCD, 2001).

For the small proportion of children with disability who have had access to education, it has generally taken place in special schools, both, state run and those managed by NGOs. The classroom pedagogies have been largely based on western models. Early intervention programmes, integrated settings and non-formal education for the disabled are recent phenomena, and exist in very small numbers. There is no country-wide documentation of such programmes. However, a record of the total umber of special schools for all ages of children is available with RCI, according to which, there are approximately 2,500 special schools that cater to nearly 1,00,000 students. Apart from that, the scheme Integrated Education of the Disabled Child of the Ministry of Human Resource Development has enrolled 60,000 children in 15,000 of its integrated schools. It is also speculated that a large number of orthopaedically and learning disabled children attend regular schools without any support services. The only speciality that seems to have taken cognizance of the significance of preschool years is that of hearing impairment. In 1990, the Ali Yavar Jung National Institute for the Hearing Handicapped at Mumbai launched a preschool movement of the hearing impaired. By 1994, it had set up 108 such programmes all over India, including in rural areas (Kundu, 2000). It provides early intervention through three types of programmes:

Age group	*Programme*
0-2 years	Parent-infant training
2-5 years	Preschool education
5-8 years	Preparatory classes

A few voluntary agencies such as the National Association for the Blind have set up preparatory schools for visually impaired children that meet the needs of children as young as preschool age. However, such initiatives are few.

Government Laws, Policies and Initiatives

The first major initiative of the Central Government that demonstrated its commitment to the welfare of the disabled was setting up of four National Institutes dealing with different areas of disability. These are:

1. National Institute for the Hearing Handicapped in Mumbai.
2. National Institute for the Mentally Handicapped in Secunderabad.
3. National Institute for the Visually Handicapped in Dehradun.
4. National Institute for the Orthopaedically Handicapped in Kolkata.

The Government administers work related to persons with

disability through the Ministry of Social Justice and Empowerment (formerly referred to as the Ministry of Welfare). This Ministry has been instrumental in enacting two important legislations that are seen as landmark steps in the empowerment of people with disability, even though these instruments have many lacunae.

The Persons with Disabilities (Equal Opportunities, Protection of Rights and Full Participation) Act, 1995, passed by the Parliament on 1st January, 1996, is an important legislation to promote the care and education of children with special needs (Ministry of Law, Justice & Company Affairs, 1996). It does so in several ways.

The Act calls upon the State to make provision for the inclusion of children in the mainstream, including preschool age children. It recommends free education for children with disabilities up to the age of 18, integration and inclusion of the children in regular schools, and provision of special schools where necessary.

[Keeping this in view, the Ministry of Human Resource Development, that deals with the subject of education in the country, has stated that the 2 million disabled children will be brought to school in 20 years (beginning with year 2000), and the majority, i.e., approximately 2 million, would receive education through regular schools with support services.]

Manpower development is another significant recommendation of this legislation. [To meet the enormous need for training rehabilitation professionals, the RCI has recognized 123 training institutions in the country to train nearly 2500 personnel per year. Of the 16 categories of professionals, special educators for all levels of school education are only one category. Preschool educators are subsumed under this head and not mentioned separately (Kundu, 2000: xxvi). In view of the emphasis on the inclusive approach, it is envisaged to orient general teachers to childhood disabilities and special education methods in pre-service training, and to provide in-service orientation to the existing teacher workforce.]

The second legislation of significance is The National Trust for Welfare of Persons with Autism, Cerebral Palsy, Mental

Retardation and Multiple Disabilities Act, 1999. Passed in December 1999 by the Indian Parliament, the primary objective of the Act is to set up a trust that would "enable and empower persons with disability to live as independently and as fully as possible within and as close to the community to which they belong." An objective that has positive implications for the young child states that the Trust shall "strengthen facilities to provide support to persons with disability to live within their own families." Thus, it would be possible for young children to receive support services nearer home (Ministry of Law, Justice & Company Affairs, 1999).

At this point let us go back to the central issue of this paper—play, and study the inevitability of its occurrence and experience for all children's optimal development.

Antecedents to Play

For play to occur freely it is necessary for some conditions to exist within and outside the child, although these may not be sufficient for its manifestation. Sutton-Smith and Roberts (1981), in their review of extensive cross-cultural research on play, delineated the antecedents of play as biological, psychological and cultural. It is relevant to consider some of these propositions here.

Discussing the *biological* antecedents of play Sutton-Smith and Roberts (1981) make reference to Peter Reynolds' "flexibility complex" hypothesis which he explains as conditions that underlie the amount of playfulness that different species demonstrate. In the human context, Reynolds reasons, there has been progressive phylogenetic expansion of the flexibility complex. That is, with delay in maturation and prolonged dependence of the human infant on parents, there is also institutionalization of play groups. Hence, playing with others is seen as a human need. The authors (Sutton-Smith and Roberts) also find support for their biological argument of play in Jerome Bruner's contention that too much motivation arousal can interfere with learning. In the context of play, Bruner is quoted as saying… "By de-emphasizing the importance of the goal, play may serve to reduce excessive drive and thus enable young animals and children to learn more easily the skill they will need when they are older" (Bruner, 1975: 82).

The two foregoing hypotheses contribute to the understanding that the human child is biologically predisposed to engage in play for natural need satisfaction and as an ontogenetic preparatory exercise for adult activity. In that sense then, play in children is a developmental prerequisite for growth towards maturity. It follows that when and if children are not able to engage in play due to reasons of disability or disorder, it has negative implications for their growth and development. Absence of playfulness in the early years has been linked with a lack of originality in later years (Anandalakshmy, 1990).

While absence of or minimal display of play is indicative of growth retardation, not being able to play deprives children of the opportunities for self-expression, vicarious gratification and lucid activity. Play and games are known to have a critical role in the socialization of aggression. Children who play and therefore, interact with agemates, are likely to know when and how much aggression is appropriate. This is one area in which children who have disability experience difficulty. They either do not develop the skills to assert themselves among peers (because they have not played enough) or they demonstrate inappropriate aggression in the form of tantrums or hostility. Lack of contact with peers, that usually occurs in play situation, accounts for many socially undesirable behaviours in children with special needs.

Play in children is also contingent upon certain psychological antecedents. Freedom to explore is essential for play to occur. The child must be free to impose his or her own idea on the environment (Sutton-Smith & Roberts, 1981). Observations of children between 2 and 6 years show that they progressively develop social skills and the tactics in solving problems that arise during social play. They argue, negotiate, hold hands, defend or turn hostile—all in play situations. Intellectual, motor or communication impairments would tend to hinder the development of these skills in children. Hence, they need assistance and guidance in developing and enhancing their abilities in the process of normalization during early childhood.

Another psychological construct that is a precursor to relaxed play activities is a sense of security. Children play freely only when they are assured of safety, protection and security. Infants' studies have shown that secure babies, as compared to insecure ones, are more exploratory in their behaviour (Yarrow, 1976). They smile, laugh and play more willingly. Children with disabilities and disorders may not always experience the self-preservation safeguards of safety and protection for them to 'risk' playing. When disability interferes in normal locomotion, balance and maintenance of posture (for example, for children with cerebral palsy and visual impairment) they would need to be assured of safety and security before they can experience a state of relaxation, and hence engage in play. If handicaps hinder play, children are likely to demonstrate deficits in thought, feeling and action (Sharma, 1989).

Typically, in any early childhood programme for children with disability, new entrants show anxiety, distress and clinging behaviour. However, as they become familiar with the environment and the educators, their potential to respond to play and learning situations begins to unfold, and they often become active play participants.

The *culture context* has been recognized as an important antecedent to play. Child's family is the first setting for play wherein the mother, and often the grandmother, the sibling or the father, evoke play responses in the infant. The importance attached by the family to play with the young child, the forms of play, and childhood related rituals and customs in the family shape play behaviour in children.

In an intervention study of infants in their homes, play was used to enhance their cognitive development (Anandalakshmy, 1990). The researcher reported that during the experiment, the involvement and interest of the mother turned out to be a crucial factor in the child's exploratory behaviour and interest in the play objects introduced. In Chaudhary's study (1995) of early communicative interaction patterns between family members and the young child, people featured in a significant way in adults' conversation with children. She observed that this pattern was woven into the child's play too. It was common for the adult to refer to an object (such as a toy) within a social context while speaking to the child about it, such as "who gave this to you"? The researchers commented that even play objects "seem to acquire a place in the complex network of social relationships that the adults are weaving for their children" (p. 159).

In an earlier study of parent-infant interactions in India (Roopnarine, Talukdar, Jain, Joshi & Srivastava, 1990), the researchers observed that for Indian parents, play was not a separate activity to be conducted with their babies. When parents held their one-year-old infants, they were more likely to display affection than to play with them. The authors explained this parent behaviour as reflecting the socio-cultural belief in "non-aggressive tendencies and search for tranquillity" (p. 672).

In sum, play must occur in the lives of all children, as it is part of a biological plan and "it is in the service of survival" (Pearce, 1986: 170). Play will occur spontaneously when there is freedom to explore and the child feels secure. In the Indian setting, a young child's play is more likely to occur in an adult mediated context, where play gets woven into a network of care related interactions between the child and the caregivers, whether parents, siblings or others. All these conditions are as applicable to a child with disability as to any other child. Hence it is the caregivers and educators in the child's environment who need to understand how to facilitate the emergence and occurrence of play in the daily life of a child with special needs.

'Teaching' Children to Play—for Development, Learning and Self-esteem

Not all children with impairments have to be 'taught' to play. Firdaus Kanga (1990), an Indian author of an autobiographical novel 'Trying to Grow' reveals that he has a rare physical condition of brittle bones. As he was growing up, not only would his bones break easily, his body did not grow beyond a child's height. At 18, he was the size of an 8 year old. As the story of his growing years unfolds, he reveals a marvellous sense of humour and narrates how he grew up playing pranks with his sister, cousins and several girlfriends even though he was tiny and mostly bound to a wheel chair. Noticeably, his parents and sibling come through as very caring and supportive in his life.

Based on principles of development, one can begin with the assumption, that all early learning is linked to effective integration of sensory and motor experience. Consequently, children who have serious impairments of the central nervous system, locomotion, vision, hearing or speech are at a disadvantage compared to their non-disabled age-peers in acquiring a working knowledge of the world around them. Hence, the attempt in facilitating play must be to encourage children to make the best use of the strengths they have. A child with lower intelligence is likely to have intact vision and hearing. Another child with locomotor disability may have normal intelligence, vision and hearing. Invariably, when a child has a disability, that seems to become the focus of attention for others, to the neglect of faculties that are normal and can be optimized for development.

In early childhood care and education (ECCE) programmes for children with disabilities and disorders, play must form the medium of most learning activities. Since the children are likely to be similar to infants and preschoolers in their mental and social ages, working through play in individual as well as small group sessions is the best approach for an educator. Trained personnel such as special educators, occupational therapists and speech therapists can engage the children in varied forms of play while conducting their activities. While doing so, it is not only the content of the activity that is important, but also the attitude and the disposition of the adult. He/She must be able to 'play' with the child, enjoy it and infect the child with that joy so that he/she also has fun. If done in an uninvolved and routine manner, the play activity will not serve its purpose.

Apart from people, play in an ECCE centre also requires play materials and equipment, play spaces and playmates.

While the usual outdoor equipment of a regular ECCE centre is good enough for children with special needs, a few modifications may be required for children with locomotor disabilities and visual impairment. A sand pit with a few safe containers and toys thrown in is a favourite children's site for outdoor play. [For a detailed study of play activities and materials the reader may refer to 'Play Activities for Young Children' by Mina Swaminathan (1984), and 'Play Activities for Preschoolers-I & II' by Indira Gandhi National Open University, (1992)].

Some examples of low cost materials that the children respond to and that enhance sensory-motor development are water colours, sheets of paper from disposable magazines and newspapers, empty plastic bottles, film roll containers and other such bottles, coloured transparent paper, water in a basin with floating and sinking objects in it and so on.

The accounts of play ideas and activities that follow are based on my experiences at the two centres of childhood education at Lady Irwin College, New Delhi, that practice the principle of inclusive education. These provide educational facilities to children who have disabilities along with non-disabled children. The Rajkumari Amrit Kaur Child Study Centre (RAKCSC) has a programme of early childhood care and education for approximately 300 children. Its components are an infant care centre for 6 months to 3 years, a play centre for children 3-4 years, a preschool for children 4-5 years, a day care for children 3 to 5 years and an after school care programme for children 5-12 years. The second programme is the Enabling Centre. It provides primary education for 40 children in the age range 5-15 years in an inclusive setting. A special feature is that it caters to the needs of children from economically disadvantaged families.

At all age levels, the two Centres have children with various types of disabilities and disorders. These include intellectual, visual and hearing impairment, cerebral palsy, locomotor disabilities, autism, speech and behaviour disorders. The nature of the child's disability never disqualifies the child for entry into the programmes—the child, or the parent did not choose it. We work with the motto that all children are educable and play is an important medium in this process.

Children with Different Disabilities do not Play Differently

The factors that should guide an educator in designing play activities are not as much related to the type of disability as they are to the strength and limitations that a child has. A child with intellectual impairment, who also has severe attentional difficulties, will need a very different approach compared to another one with a similar disability, say Down syndrome, but who has a fairly good attention span. The ensuing discussion will be using the categories of disability outlined in the beginning of this chapter. These are not necessarily universal and can be contested by other professionals and affected persons.

In any ECCE programme for children with disabilities, the category of children with intellectual impairment is likely to be the largest. There will be those with developmental delays, so that mental retardation is not yet a confirmed diagnosis. Those with Down Syndrome and other etiologies of intellectual impairments would be with mild, moderate or severe levels of retardation. Many of them have associated impairments of vision, hearing and speech.

Intellectual impairment does not preclude the affinity for play in children. However, their play interests are likely to be typical of children much younger than them chronologically. Preschoolers may enjoy the activities that generally infants engage in. Thus playing with things they can safely mouth, chew and bang will occur. The educator needs to have the same materials in her classroom as she would have for any ECCE programme. Only, she will have to use a slower pace to interact with each child individually as well as in small groups in play-like situations, and use her skills of music, dance and drama to invite the children's participation in play. In a good programme, the boundary between play and learning activity must be flexible, the goal being to socialize the child, build her/his self-esteem and develop social and emotional competence.

Many children with delayed development have difficulty in simple activities like walking, running, jumping and balancing. Such children refrain from participating in movement activities and outdoor play. They must be given physical support and a sense of safety for play experienced such as see-saws and swings. According to Mullan (1984), movement is the very centre of children's life and "in order to enhance children's knowledge of their spatial world, we should involve them in movement activities designed to contribute to their body awareness, directional awareness and spatial awareness" (p. 11).

Group Play

Here is an account of how an educator encourages the children for play when outdoors, based on observations made by Parul, a Child Development student, at the RAKCSC. The teacher Ms. Shashi has 12 children with different disabilities in her class in the age range 4 to 7 years. Parul comments about play in Ms. Shashi's class named Saryu. She writes:

> Play in Saryu is encouraged regularly by the educators and enjoyed thoroughly by the children. In the daily routine the children spend time outdoors playing for nearly an hour, their faourite play equipments being the see-saw and the merry-go-round. Some like to sit on the ground and engage in solitary play.

Writing specifically about how Ms. Shashi makes learning of motor skills fun through play, giving at the same time a feeling of safety, Parul says:

> Ms. Shashi made effort to encourage play in children and incorporated some kind of learning as seen in the following examples. She helped Jay overcome his fear of walking without help on a row of bricks which also enhanced his sense of coordination. She made him hold her hands and walk reciting a poem side by side. After 2-3 trials Jay was able to walk half-way himself holding on tightly to his own shorts.

The student trainee finds that:

> Not only outdoor, play is encouraged even indoor in the session of free play where loads of items like balls, phones, dupattas, blocks etc. were given to the children. This helped them in imaginative play as seen when the children put the phones to their ears and pretended that they were talking to their parents or friends.

Physiotherapy and occupational therapy sessions can easily be conducted through play activities. During her observations Parul found that the occupational therapist carried out a session of play through which he encouraged the children to do activities to enhance their motor-coordination.

He kept a bucket in the centre while the children stood around it, a little away. Turn by turn he asked each child to throw a ball into the bucket. He also played a session of football with them wherein Sameer, with an orthopedic disability, was encouraged to at least touch his foot to the ball.

At the end of her observations Parul commented that overall, every moment of play was cherished by each child.

Let us take a look at guided play among slightly older children at the Enabling Centre. These observations were done by Pooja as part of her training about children with special needs. She writes:

> It was noticed that largely, play is guided by the educators. They try to include the disabled children into play activities, mainly because, unlike the other children, they were unable to occupy themselves with such pleasurable activities.

Giving an example of how the educators at The Enabling Centre enhance various skills among children through organized games, Pooja writes:

> The game was an interesting form of race. The children were divided into two teams. One member from each team was to run and compete with the other. The task was to

> dip a towel in water kept in a bucket separately for each team at the starting point, run with it to the other end where another empty bucket was kept, squeeze out the water from the towel into this bucket and then run back to the starting point with the towel. At the end, when both teams had done their laps, the water in the two buckets was measured using a glass. The team that collected more water was declared the winner.

More than 50 per cent children in the teams were those with disabilities and came from low income families. In Pooja's view, together they:

- exercised their fine-motor and gross-motor skills in squeezing the towel and running;
- learnt to follow instructions and rules;
- gained an idea of measurement;
- experienced a team spirit; and above all
- thoroughly enjoyed the game.

In her observation notes on play at RAKCSC, Pooja writes:

> The educators made conscious efforts to make play-time a fruitful learning experience for the children. It was interesting to see how the educators involved the children in fun-filled play. For example, the teacher would say:

"Come children let us walk on this row of bricks".

"Let us jump from these steps."

"Hey, come and see, who is hiding in the tunnel? I'll stand on the other side, the children will walk through the tunnel and come towards Aunty". Ms. Shashi makes the experience on the swings too enjoyable, encouraging the children also to sing along. When roughly translated the song goes like this... "little little raindrops... I swing when it rains".

Pooja gives the example of how the educator handles a child's fear who is reluctant to go through the tunnel, a pipe placed in the play area. She notes: "Ms. Shashi said to the child, Jay go... see it is okay... we all are going in".

Jay refused to go in. Respecting the child's fear, the teacher did not force him to enter the tunnel. But, she tried to talk to him very gently, almost everyday thereafter. She was positive that he will overcome his fear if prepared gradually.

Individualized Work Through Play

Working individually with children who have disabilities is a necessary part of special education. When the child is new in the programme or is moved to another group, establishing rapport before any work begins is essential. At the education centres at Lady Irwin College, the students of Child Development learn to do individual work with children.

As part of this exercise, they first familiarize themselves to them. Quite often, the process of rapport formation itself is quite challenging for the students. Play methodology is quite handy in these situations. An illustration would help in explaining how this is done.

Prateek had intellectual impairment and behaviour disorder when he joined RAKCSC. Observations revealed a very low attention span, difficulty with memory, thought and speech. He would hit, bite and abuse children quite frequently. The other children were petrified of him. Rekha, a student, was assigned to work with him and write his case study. Whenever Prateek started to run, Rekha ran after him pretending that he was running too fast and she could not catch him. She allowed him to dodge her for a while. He started enjoying the game and interactions between the two started off. Prateek started seeking out Rekha to play with her. Apparently, rapport had been established.

Children like Prateek, who are distractible and hyperactive, give a tough time to educators who keep trying to persuade the child to be seated for a while and do some work with paper and pencil. Rekha tried some interesting activities to elicit Prateek's interest and increase his on-seat behaviour. By now Prateek was 6 years old. Rekha devised a cat-and-mouse game to encourage him to hold a crayon and draw. On a drawing sheet she drew figures of several cats on the one end and equal number of mice opposite them, as Prateek could recognize both these figures and label them.

Fig. 4.1: Cat and mouse game

Rekha gave him a crayon and told him to draw one line from the cat to the mouse opposite it if she clapped once. If she clapped twice, he was to draw two lines. Prateek could understand the instructions and played the game repeatedly, asking Rekha to take her turn at drawing lines while he clapped. He could play this game for 10 to 20 minutes with a few distractions.

In another self-devised game involving the use of paper and pencil (or crayon) Rekha taught Prateek to write the letter A. It started as a story about a bird that was hungry and had to walk some distance to find its food.

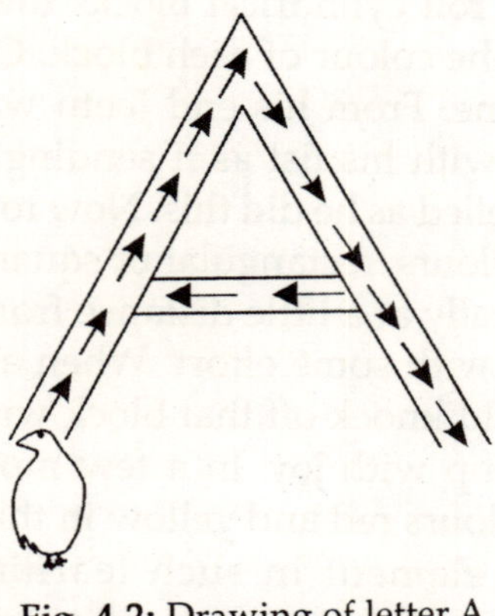

Fig. 4.2: Drawing of letter A

As shown in the figure Prateek was led along the shape of the letter 'A' saying that the bird found some grains on top and later located some more below and then again on the side, so as to complete the form of the letter 'A'. While Prateek was following this on his sheet of paper, on a separate sheet, Rekha copied Prateek's hand movements and said, "Oh! This looks like A to me doesn't it?" To this Prateek responded with an excited laughter, picked up his sheets and went around telling the teachers and the children, "See it looks like A". Gradually Prateek's attention span improved and in six-month time he could sit up to half-an-hour to attend to tasks.

Working with severely disabled children, special educators can devise innovative ways of playing with them so that they learn important concepts. The play-way method of learning was very beautifully seen in the case of Jeetu who had joined the Centre as a 6-year old with quadriplegia. He could not sit, had no head control and speech was absent, but he seemed to comprehend quite a bit. He had a lively face and expressive eyes which he could use to communicate some of his needs and emotions. His teachers talked to him, included him in all the activities to the extent possible and tried to teach him some concepts. But, they found it difficult to assess if he had acquired any cognitive concepts.

One of the educators devised a way of teaching Jeetu the colour concept. She discovered that he could move his forearm 3-4 inches when resting on a table in front. She would sit opposite him and roll cylindrical blocks towards him on the table, telling him the colour of each block. Only three colours were used at a time. From his end Jeetu was encouraged to 'push' the blocks with his fist as if sending them back. Each one was again labelled as he did this. Now to test if Jeetu could recall any of the colours, rectangular or square coloured blocks were placed vertically at a little distance from Jeetu so that he could reach them with some effort. When asked to show the red block, he would knock off that block with his fist and his eyes would light-up with joy. In a few months, Jeetu could clearly identify colours red and yellow in this way.

An essential element in such learning-through-play situations has been the presence of a non-authoritarian, motivated and caring adult, who is sensitive to the child's moods and acts like a playmate.

Children with Visual and Hearing Impairments

Play for children with sensory deficits, that is, visual impairments and hearing loss requires special attention. Those who can see only partially or are blind have to be helped to become familiar with the physical space, the furniture and the people around them so that they are assured of safety. They will respond to toys and materials through touch and sound. Thus, balls and dolls with bells inside that make interesting sounds are good examples of toys for them. Use of participatory drama in enacting stories with visually impaired children was found to be an exciting way of teaching them by Richa, a master's student, conducting her research (Tyagi, 1999). She taught 7 and 8 year olds sense of direction through play activities such as rhythmic body movements with music. When children acted as soldiers looking for the king's moustache in a story 'The king has lost his moustache', they discovered that the spaces around them had names such as left, right, forward and backward.

A child who cannot hear does not necessarily have different play needs. However, inability to hear and use speech may cause the child to be isolated among peers. Taking care of the child's social needs would be an important factor while promoting play. If hearing loss is mild to moderate and goes unnoticed in the early years, as is often the case, it can lead to behaviour difficulties in children. One such child was Mala, who showed aggression towards her peers. At 3 years Mala was admitted in the regular class as the parents did not mention anything unusual about her. Very soon, the teacher discovered that Mala was not responding to verbal communication nor did she show interest in language activities. She had very little speech, mostly incomprehensible. Assessment of hearing at different clinics indicated no hearing loss. However, since Mala showed behavioural response of a partially deaf child at the preschool, it was considered judicious to treat her as at least pseudo-deaf and work accordingly. Mala did not have friends and resisted any individualized attention. While work in another area of development was in progress, play situations were created to foster sociability in her. The student trainee devised several games of which two are described below:

- *Playing with ball*: The trainee took Mala outdoors with a few children and gave them a football to play. Mala first refused to play ball with any other person except the trainee. A little cajoling and she agreed to allow one more child to play the game. The next time her permission was sought to include a few more of her peers. Mala was made the leader who would give turns to other children. She responded positively to these play situations and began to participate in peer interactions even in her classroom.
- *Joining dots*: Dots were made on a paper at a little distance from one another in the form of a simple design. Mala and two other children were shown how they could take turns at joining the dots to make a figure. At first Mala refused to co-operate. But she found that the other children were enjoying the game, and she also joined in. This way she acquired a few social skills and verbal expressions that accompany children's interactions.

After nearly a year and a half of work with her, a formal hearing assessment by the hospital that had declared her 'not-deaf', reported a moderate hearing loss, a factor that had guided our programme for her.

Children with Autism

Autism is a behavioural syndrome that is attributed to brain abnormalities and dysfunction (Hynd & Hooper, 1992). It may be present from the very beginning in the child or may develop after a few years of normal development. The child has certain typical behaviour characteristics that fall under three categories.

(i) Social abnormalities include lack of responsiveness to other people, lack of eye contact, resistance to approach by others and absence of play, especially symbolic play.

(ii) Language abnormalities are reflected in either absence of speech, or if present, there is lack of conversational ability, delayed echolalia and use of pronominal reversals.

(iii) Stereotyped repetitive patterns in behaviour such as self stimulation, abnormal preoccupations and abnormal attachment to objects.

Engaging autistic children in play activities is one of the most difficult tasks that educators faced. Their preference for staying aloof makes them poor partners in any attempts at play. However, intervention through play is a therapeutic procedure to develop desirable social and personal skills in children with autism.

Work with an autistic boy at the Enabling Centre provides a rare glimpse into this teaching-learning of play.

Tushar (12 years) had been at the Centre for a year when he was observed by Smita, a post-graduate student, as part of her case study work. He belonged to a middle class nuclear family and had one younger sibling. After assessing the child and forming rapport with him, Smita planned her intervention strategies, some of which were play-based. She found out through her observations that Tushar's play activities were restricted to repetitive actions with objects and there was total absence of constructive and imaginative play. However, he was fond of music, something that a lot of children with autism show.

Smita decided to introduce 'learning to play' with emphasis on developing initiative in cooperative games. One was a game that was accompanied with a rhyme and the other was a card game. The strategies she worked out for herself were:

- Be flexible—adjust plans to suit the child's needs and interest.
- Take turns with the child in action, object manipulation and speech.

- ➢ Demonstrate action—be dramatic!
- ➢ Comment on your own action and those of the child.
- ➢ Give verbal directions.
- ➢ Provide regular reinforcement.

A. *Rhyme Game*: The rhyme that is recited while playing this indoor game is traditionally known in most Hindi speaking regions. It goes like this, *"Akkar bakkar bambay bo, assi nabbe poorey sau"*...

Two or more participants sit facing one another or in a semi-circle with their hands on a flat surface like a table or even the floor, fingers spread out. Starting with one person's little finger, the leader (whose one hand is also in the table) starts reciting the rhyme and with every word moves from one finger to the next tapping each one till the end of the four line rhyme. Wherever the rhyme ends, the finger is folded in by its owner. Thus the person who has his/her last finger still out, when all other are in, is the winner.

Smita involved Tushar in this game, though he had to be guided and verbally instructed. She encouraged him to take turns at tapping the fingers, in timing the tapping with the rhyme and in verbalizing the words of the rhyme.

B. *Card Game*: This game required a pack of cards. Tushar was required to recognize two matching cards in the game. He had the ability to recognize numbers and pictures on the cards. He was first made familiar with the fact that the same number or picture could appear on different cards. The game involved Smita and Tushar. The procedure was as follows:

- ➢ Place anyone card with its face up.
- ➢ Divide the remaining pack into two piles, each player taking one pile.
- ➢ Take turns to throw a card on the top of the first card.

- As soon as a card matching the one facing is thrown, the player puts his/her hand on all the cards and wins them.
- The game starts again.
- One who has more cards is the winner.

In the beginning Tushar would not stop the game even if he had thrown a matching card. Smita encouraged him to make eye contact with his matching card and identify the similarity. To facilitate his understanding she broke the game into a series of steps. As soon as the matching card was thrown by Tushar, she would place a bright red paper on the card and ask him to take away the cards he had won. Tushar did not have an awareness of winning. Even if he was given the card 'won' by him, he showed no excitement or joy. Smita taught him to clap with her whenever anyone 'won'. Clapping brought him cheer.

Tushar seemed to enjoy this game as he was ready to play it whenever Smita went to work with him.

At the end of several sessions with these two games Smita concluded that Tushar:

- Could understand rules
- Could imitate her actions
- Could take turns
- Could follow use of markers to end of one stage
- Could not comprehend the concept of winning and losing
- Seemed to enjoy the two games

The domains of Tushar's development on which Smita observed positive effects were:

- *Cognition*: counting, matching numbers and figures
- *Language*: learning of rhymes, sentence formation, clarity of speech
- *Socialization*: reciprocal interaction

Many children with autism respond well to games that are suitable for typical children of younger age, such as games that involve the sense of touch, rhythmic patting, tickling and gentle pinch. Since many of them make monotonous rocking movements, these can be used as a starting point to develop them into real dancing movements for those who may be willing. A child who insists on walking around cannot be held back physically from doing this. But if surprising him (peek-a-boo) or singing a song along or imitating him and laughing produces a variation, the child may begin to enjoy it and demand more.

The strategies that work well while teaching play skills to children with autism are:

(i) Use of the parallel play approach
(ii) Following the child's lead, focusing attention on objects and activities selected by the child where possible
(iii) Imitating the child's action as a starting point
(iv) Taking turns with the child, sometimes giving physical prompts
(v) Demonstrating to the child the action you want him or her to use
(vi) Commenting on your own actions and those of the child
(vii) Providing positive reinforcement, using rewards that please the child

A precaution that needs to be observed when playing with autistic children is that the adult must retreat as soon as the child shows a wish to withdraw. For example, if a fear response becomes apparent, reduce the 'boo' part in the 'peek-a-boo' game. Avoid an all intrusive approach, including even looking straight at the child. Let go for a while and resume only when the child shows he is ready. Be prepared to repeat a game time and again. The adult may be tired of it, but the child often is not and likes the ritual. Adding a variation or a new game may make it possible to gradually drop the stale game.

Children with Behavioural and Emotional Disturbance

There is a view in recent texts that the terms behavioural and emotional can be used interchangeably as they refer to practically the same expressions in children (Smith & Luckasson, 1995). Emotional disturbance in a child can primarily be inferred through behaviour and all behaviour problems have an emotional context. Young children show some emotional problems some of the time during the developmental years. However, a few may become victims of their stressful circumstances, at home or away from home, such that they display unusual levels of disturbance in their behaviours. In preschool years these may be expressed overtly in the form of aggression, fears and phobias etc. or may be internalized, as in withdrawal from social contact. In her classical book 'Play Therapy' Virginia Axline (1947) had outlined the innovative use of play to treat children with varied emotional problems.

Play has been found to have an important role in therapy of children who are disturbed. As a general rule, the younger the child, the more likely that play techniques will be successful in therapy, as a tool play facilitates emotional expression and allows communication between the therapist (or educator) and the child. Since children younger than seven do not usually have the precision of language or the verbal labels to communicate their emotions, play opportunities serve as ideal ground for diagnosis as well as therapy for the problems they are facing. Even if a child can verbalize, he/she may be uncomfortable in talking face to face with an adult, and play activities make for a comfortable barrier between child and adult.

It is not necessary for an educator to be a trained psychotherapist in order to use play opportunities for therapeutic purposes. Teachers who are keen learners can be good therapists with some training. A lot of the material that ECCE programmes usually have is quite adequate for designing play therapy sessions. A few dolls and a dolls' house is a must. Observant teachers will make use of indoor and outdoor activity times to reach out to a disturbed child through play. Usually, play therapy is an indirect method whereby the focus is on the particular play activity and not directly on the emotional conflict. The results of this form of treatment may be visible immediately or very slowly, varying from child to child.

When provided with toys and materials that can be manipulated by the child at will, he or she may play with them in a way that sources of disturbance can be located. Such play situations serve the projective function in diagnosis. The child must be allowed to feel free to say anything, order about his/her fantasy characters, be slow or fast, express hate or love or be indifferent without being censured by the adult. Both action and verbalization of the child in this process can reveal feelings of confusion, anger, frustration, stress, fear, insecurity etc. By playing out these emotions openly, the child brings them to the surface and feels emotional relaxation, a kind of catharsis. The educator, who has been an observer, can intervene at critical junctures, ask a few questions while play proceeds and gather her data for diagnosis and play intervention.

Play was used effectively for diagnosis and therapy at RAKCSC by Gurman, a student trainee, for a 4-year-old boy Sarthak. His teacher reported that he showed frequent unprovoked aggression towards peers and adults and had low compliance to her requests. Gurman conducted several observations of Sarthak's behaviour using the time sampling technique to study the pattern of his aggression.

Along with observations, three doll play sessions were also carried out with him. These revealed important information about his home and family members. Some of the events that took place are thus.

Session I

Sarthak placed two dolls in the dolls' house and filled up the rest of the space with blocks and utensils. He said (in Hindi), pointing at the two dolls, "This is Sarthak and this is Ina" (his younger sister).

Gurman asked, "And this one?" (pointing to the dolls kept outside the doll house).

Sarthak: "These dolls don't live there, two are enough."

Gurman: "So this is Sarthak, and Mama Papa?"

Sarthak picked up a doll that wore a bindi and said, "This is Mama?"

Gurman: "Where does she live?"

Sarthak put the doll on the roof and said, "Here".

Gurman: "Where have you put Mama?"

Sarthak: "On top".

Gurman: "Why is she on top?"

Sarthak: "Mama can see everything from the top".

After a brief pause, Sarthak removed the Mama doll, put it on the floor and said, "Remove Mama, there is no one else at home". After a while, he pointed to the one legged doll and said, "This one without a leg is Mama".

Session II

There were two doll houses, one large and one small. Gurman pointed to the bigger house and asked: "Who will live in this?"

Sarthak: "Dadi (grandmother), Baba (grandfather), Mama and Sarthak".

Gurman: "And Papa?"

Sarthak: "Here (pointing to the smaller doll house)."

He picked up a doll and put it in the small house. He then picked up a toy gun and placed it next to this doll.

Gurman: "What is this?"

Sarthak: "Guest house".

Gurman: "Papa sleeps in the guest house? Not with you?"

Sarthak: "When a thief comes then Papa kills him".

In all three sessions, Sarthak placed the gun next to one doll or another and talked of killing thieves with guns.

In the third session, Sarthak said that the dolls' house was equipped with switches which, when pressed, threw out bombs through the roof.

Thus problems related to parent-child and mother-father relationships emerged in Sarthak's fantasy play. There also were several indicators of latent anger and hostility. Sarthak's teacher and school counsellor had several meetings with the parents (of course, without revealing the context of play observations) to discuss Sarthak's behaviour.

A strategy to modify Sarthak's behaviour towards peers

was worked out by Gurman and his teacher. It was decided to evolve a story in the class using puppets. Apart from the fact that children identify easily with toys, using puppets gives them the anonymity they need to bring out their feelings. Secure in the knowledge that they cannot be blamed for what the puppet said, they can delve deeply into the very complex problems forming family relationships, and at the same time maintain their dignity and self-respect.

There were a set of puppets that the teachers in the preschool used for puppet shows on different themes. Sarthak's teacher and Gurman decided that a puppet show would be held in front of the whole group of 20 children and all of them, including Sarthak, would be involved in developing a story. As an innovation, it was decided to have a balloon puppet as the main character in the story 'Golu ki kahani' (Golu's story). This would permit several variations such as holding Golu with a thread, enlarging or reducing its size or discussing the risk of its bursting. The gentle mobility of the balloon made Golu appear unique as a puppet.

Golu was introduced as a little boy who troubled other boys in a nursery. He would hit, push, pinch, pull them and do all kinds of mischievous things. A total of three episodes were conducted over three days in which the children were encouraged to add to the story. In the second and third episodes an attempt was made to bring out a slight change in Golu's behaviour—to make it more socially desirable.

In the first episode, Golu starts losing his air and requests the other toys to fill him up, otherwise "he will die". When Gurman asked the children if air should be filled up to keep him alive, they said "yes". Sarthak initially said "no", but later agreed with the other children. On being asked what will happen if Golu again did bad things, Sarthak said, "Then we will take his air out". After the second episode, when the children were asked if naughty children could become better, all the children said "yes, they could", but Sarthak said, "no, they cannot become better". By the third episode, Sarthak suggested ways to turn Golu into a good boy and wanted to take the balloon home.

Later, when Gurman visited Sarthak's home his

grandmother said that Sarthak had often referred to himself as Golu saying "Golu will do this", "Golu will do that".

Neena—A Withdrawn Child

Investigative therapeutic use of play was made in the case of Neena, a 3 year-old girl at the preschool. Her teacher reported that Neena was extremely tense and remained apathetic to her environment. Neena was the eldest of three children, the younger two being boys. It was also revealed that both parents treated Neena as a child old enough not to be cuddled, were punitive in their handling and referred to her as a 'difficult' child. The mother admitted that she had not been able to give enough attention to Neena as the other two children arrived within two years after her.

Observations revealed that Neena could comprehend at her age-level but her speech was incoherent, sentences disconnected and incomplete. Ritu, the student-trainee, first formed a working relationship with Neena. One day she persuaded her to come to the activity room where a lot of play materials were laid out. Neena first stood at the door very sceptically and asked, whether she would be punished if she touched any of the toys. When Ritu assured her that she had freedom to do what she liked, she gingerly touched and manipulated some toys. She got interested in the dolls' house. Within a few minutes Neena started talking continuously. She assigned different dolls the identity of her family members but left out her brother next to her in birth order. On earlier occasions too, Neena verbalized rivalry towards this sibling.

Through 20 minutes of make-belief play with dolls that morning, Neena conveyed to Ritu her emotional state, the punitiveness of her parents, the mother's neglect and rejection towards her, sibling rivalry and her craving for the mother's affection. She talked about her sleep disturbance and her unwillingness to attend school. Subsequently Ritu used guided doll play with Neena and other strategies to resolve some of her conflicts. Neena's parents too received counselling sessions. Gradually Neena became more relaxed and sociable. She stayed at the preschool for two years and jointed an elementary school at age 5 as a playful child.

Conclusion

The Indian scenario for young children with special needs, at this juncture, appears quite dismal. Several million need immediate attention, care, treatment and education. While treatment and education services require professional intervention and will, therefore, take longer to reach all children, it is quality care and attention that can be available to practically all children, as these are family based activities. In fact, its absence or diminished display in environments where children with disabilities are growing up, serves to signal risk to development and warrants appropriate action for intervention.

REFERENCES

Anandalakshmy, S. (1990). Enhancing cognitive development: Stimulation play infancy. In U. Bevli (Ed.), *Research in Child Development: A book of readings* (pp. 100-113). New Delhi: National Council for Educational Research and Training.

Axline, V.M. (1947). *Play therapy.* New York: Ballantine Books.

Bruner, J. (1975). Play is a serious business. *Psychology Today.* 8, 81-83.

Chaturvedi, S.K. & Malhotra, S. (1984). A follow up study of mental retardation focusing on parental attitudes. *Indian Journal of Psychiatry*. 26, 370-376.

Chaudhary, N. (1995). *Family interaction patterns and language development in infancy*. Unpublished doctoral dissertation, Department of Home Science, University of Delhi, Delhi.

Chaudhary, N. (1999). Language socialization: Patterns of caregiver speech to young children. In T.S. Saraswathi (Ed.), *Culture, socialization and human development* (pp. 145-166). New Delhi: Sage.

Dalal, A.K. & Pandey, N. (1999). Cultural beliefs and family care of the children with disability. *Psychology and Developing Societies*. 11 (1), 55-75.

Fleer, M. (1996). Theories of 'play': Are they ethnocentric or inclusive? *Australian Journal of Early Childhood*, 21 (4), 12-17.

Garvey, C. (1977). *Play*. United Kingdom: Fontana Open Books.

Hutt, C. (1976). Exploration and play in children. In J. Bruner, A. Jolly, & K. Sylva (Eds.), Play. New York: Penguin.

Hynd, G. W. & Hooper, S.R. (1992). *Neurological basis of childhood psychopathology*. New Delhi: Sage.

Indian Council for Child Welfare. (1994). *Rights of the Child: Report of a National Consultation*. New Delhi: ICCW.

Indira Gandhi National Open University. (1992). *Play activities for preschoolers-I & II*. Course material for 'Organizing Child Care Services' of Diploma in Early Childhood Education, School of Continuing Education, New Delhi: IGNOU.

Joshi, P. (2001). *The meaning of disability: Experiences and expressions from children's lives*. Unpublished doctoral dissertation, Department of Home Science, University of Delhi, Delhi.

Kanga, F. (1990). *Trying to grow*. Delhi: Ravi Dayal.

Kandu, C.L. (Ed.) (2000). Status of disability in India. 2000. New Delhi: Rehabilitation Council of India.

Lowenfeld, M. (1935). Play in childhood. London: Victor Gollancz.

Leve, R.M. (1995). *Child and adolescent psychotherapy*. Boston: Allyn & Bacon.

Mehra, V. (1995). *Parental perceptions and patterns of young children's play*. Unpublished master's thesis, Department of Home Science, University of Delhi, Delhi.

Ministry of Law, Justice and Company Affairs. (1996). *The persons with disabilities (Equal opportunities, protection of rights and full participation) Act, 1995*. New Delhi: Government of India.

Ministry of Law, Justice and Company Affairs. (1999). *The national trust for welfare of persons with autism, Cerebral palsy. Mental Retardation and Multiple Disabilities Act, 1999*. New Delhi: Government of India.

Mullan, M.R. (1984). Motor development and children's play. In T.D. Yawkey & A.D. Pellegrini (Eds.) *Child's play and play therapy* (pp. 7-15). Pennsylvania: Technomic Publishing Co.

Navalkar, P. (2001). *Father's perception of his role in parenting* a *child with cerebral palsy*. Unpublished M.Phil dissertation, Tata Institute of Social Sciences, Mumbai.

National Institute of Public Cooperation and Child Development. (2001). Draft national policy on education for children with disabilities by RCI. Paper circulated at the *National Workshop on Inclusive Education for Children with Disabilities: Prospects and Challenges*. 7-8 November, New Delhi: NIPCCD.

Pal. R. (1991). *The autistic child in the Indian family*. Unpublished master's thesis, Department of Home Science, University of Delhi, Delhi.

Pandey, R.S. & Advani, L. (1996). *Perspectives in disability and rehabilitation*. New Delhi: Vikas Publishing House.

Parten, M.B. (1932). Social participation among preschool children. *Journal of Abnormal and Social Psychology*, 27, 243-269.

Pearce, J.E. (1986). *Magical Child*. Toronto: Bantam Books.

Phoolka, R. (1990) *Family dynamics in homes of young children with sensory deficits*. Unpublished master's thesis, Department of Home Science, University of Delhi, Delhi.

Piaget, J. (1962). *Play, dreams and limitation in childhood*. New York: Norton.

Roopnarine, J.L., Talukdar, E., Jain, D., Joshi, P., & Srivastava, P. (1990). Characteristics of holding, patterns of play and social behaviours between parents and infants in New Delhi, India *Developmental Psychology*, 26(4), 667-673.

Registrar General of India. (2001). *Census of India* (On line) http://www.censusindia.net

Sen, A. (1988). *Psycho-social integration of the handicapped: A challenge to the society*. New Delhi: Mittal Publications.

Sharma, N. (1989). *Infant stimulation: Documentation of research in Delhi*. Unpublished report. New Delhi: UNICEF.

Smith, D.D. & Luckasson, R. (1995). *Introduction to special education* (2nd ed.). Boston: Allyn and Bacon.

Sutton-Smith, B. & Roberts, J.M. (1981). Play, games and sports. In H.C. Triandis & A. Heron (Eds.) *Handbook of cross-cultural developmental psychology: Vol. 4* (pp. 425-471). Boston: Allyn and Bacon.

Swaminathan, M. (1984). *Play activities for young children*. Chennai: UNICEF.

Tyagi, R. (1999). *Drama and stories in the education of visually impaired children*. Unpublished master's thesis, Department of Home Science, University of Delhi, Delhi.

Vygotsky, L.S. (1981). The genesis of higher mental functions. In IV. Wertsch (Ed.), *The concept of activity in Soviet psychology* (pp. 145-172). Arrnonk, NY: r1.E. Sharpe.

Yarrow, Ls.I (1976). *Infant and environment*. New York: Hemisphere.

5

An Indian Model of Early Childhood Education and Development in a Nepalese Context

KISHORE SHRESTHA

Organized and concerted efforts to expand Early Childhood Care and Education (ECCE) services in Nepal is relatively a recent phenomenon. Management of ECCE does not fall under the formal structure of any of the ministries of the government. As the existing ECCE is not part of the mainstream government programme, the government has not allocated any fund for ECCE in its regular budget. ECCE in Nepal is accessible only to a limited number of children and confined to urban areas.

In the 1990s, Early Childhood Care and Education received unprecedented attention and concern in Nepal. In response to the commitments made by His Majesty's Government of Nepal in the international forums—the UN Convention on the Rights of the Child (1989), the World Summit for Children (1999), and the World Conference on Education for All (1999)—national plans and policies for ECCE have been developed and various ECCE programmes have been implemented.

The neighbouring country, India, has a long history of ECCE services. Since its independence in 1947, ECCE has been a constant focus for all major commissions and development plans of the Government of India, as a result of Integrated Child Development Services (ICDS) scheme.

The ICDS programme is one of the major comprehensive ECCE programmes implemented in India. This is one of the largest child development programmes in the world (World Bank, 1996). This programme demonstrates how a developing country with very low-income levels can manage to spend substantially and on a national scale for the welfare of the children. With regard to ICDS, Heaver and Hunt (1995) write, "India, whose Integrated Child Development Services programme now covers most of the country's most disadvantaged children, is an example of what can be achieved despite low per capita income" (p. 28). Despite a number of drawbacks and limitations and huge challenges ahead, ICDS has received wide appreciation. It has become the largest programme of its kind in the world (Myers, 1993). The Ministry of Human Resource Development, Government of India in its Annual Report (1995) states—"Integrated Child Development Services Scheme (ICDS) which is described as the country's gift to our children [children of India] is today the world's largest and most widely acclaimed child development programme" (p. 9).

This paper is based on the assumption that a country like Nepal with relatively low resources available for ECCE should learn from the experiences of the neighbouring country whose socio-economic background is, to a large extent, similar. This paper has three main sections. The first section deals with the attributes of the Integrated Child Development Services (ICDS) programme of India. The second section deals with the background information on Nepal and situation of Early Childhood Care and Education in Nepal. The third section deals with the lessons that Nepal can learn from the Indian experiences in delivering ECCE services to children living in disadvantaged situations.

Major Attributes of ICDS Programme

Some of the major attributes of the ICDS programme that a developing country like Nepal to learn are as follows:

Targeted to Children Belonging to Poor Families and Living in Disadvantaged Situations

The Integrated Child Development Services Programme in India caters to the need of rural and disadvantaged children from pre-natal stage to 6 years of age. Health, Nutrition and Education related services are provided free of cost. Although the communities have both the rich and poor people, only the poor families avail of the services. The programme is providing basic health, nutrition and early stimulation services to more than 20 million children belonging to poor economic strata and living in rural and disadvantaged situation.

Involvement of Various Governmental Ministries, Line Agencies, National Organizations in the Implementation of the Programme

The ICDS programme is sponsored centrally, but implemented by the States. Various ministries (e.g. Ministry of Human Resource Development, Ministry of Health etc.) and national organizations are involved in planning, coordination and implementation of the project. Co-ordination is achieved at various government levels (Centre, State/Union Territory), and the district, block and village levels. The project personnel and the health personnel jointly run the programme at village level.

To ensure effective co-ordination and co-operation among various ministries, departments, organizations and local bodies, Co-ordination Committees are formed at different levels.

The health component is mentioned at the Central level by All India Institute of Medical Sciences, at the state level by the state directorates of health department and at the project level by the primary health centres.

The National Institute of Public Co-operation and Child Development (NIPCCD) is the apex organization involved in providing training to programme personnel.

Training for Child Development Programme Officers (CDPOs) and supervisors of ICDS programme is directly provided by this organization. It also conducts orientation programmes for senior officers involved in the ICDS programme. The Anganwadi Workers (AWs) are trained by voluntary organizations, such as the Indian Council for Child Welfare and its state branches, on the basis of the syllabus developed by NIPCCD.

The Programme Includes Health, Nutrition and Early Childhood Education for the Holistic Development of Children

For the holistic development of the child, the ICDS scheme has integrated the programmes of health, nutrition and early childhood education, and extended its services to the children in the age group of 0 to 6 years and their mothers. Mothers have been made an integral part of the programme and equal recipients of the programme benefits (Sadka, 1984). Its package of services includes supplementary nutrition, immunization, health check up, referral services, non-formal pre-school education, and nutrition and health education for children below six years, and to pregnant and nursing mothers (Murlidharan & Kaul, 1993).

The concept of providing an integrated service for child growth and development is based on three major assumptions. Firstly, the total impact of the programme would be greater if all the important services are delivered in an integrated way than the sum of their separate effects. It is so because the efficiency of a particular service depends upon the support it receives from related services. Secondly, delivery of the services tends to be cost effective due to the cut-off in the duplication of services. Thirdly, it is administratively feasible to provide services in an integrated manner.

The Programme is Targeted to Children from Conception to Below Six Years of Age

The programme accepts the view that the development of a child begins from the conception and early development has profound effect on children's later lives. The programme covers a wide range of health, nutrition and education services for the welfare of the children and mothers. Provision of health and nutrition education to all women betwen 15 to 45 years of age, and provision of health check-ups, immunization and supplementary nutrition services to the pregnant and nursing women indicate that the programme has taken into consideration the development of child from the conception to the age of 6. However, in terms of early stimulation, the programme does not include any input for children below 3 years of age.

Such a wide range of service recipients under a single programme is a unique characteristic of the ICDS programme.

Financing of Programme

Unlike governments in many other developing countries, the Government of India is financing ECCE programmes from the national budget. The Central Government and the State/Union Territory Governments concerned share expenses on Government-run ECCE centres. Resources from various NGOs and international donor agencies are also availed. The ICDS programme is funded by the Central Government. However, State Governments also subscribe funds to meet the costs of supplementary nutrition programme. Funds are also channelled from international donor agencies for the programme.

In Spite of being a Low Cost Programme it has Demonstrated Significant Achievements in Certain Important Indicators of Child Development

Despite being a centrally funded project with virtually no local and user contribution, it is interesting to note that the programme is found to be the most cost effective. The total cost of the programme is only about US $ 10 per child annually (Kaul, 1993). It was estimated (in 1984) that all children in India could enjoy the ICDS services at a total administrative cost of 0.65 per cent of the GDP (Sadka, 1984).

The evaluation of the programme reveals a positive impact on the health and nutrition status of mothers and children, and on general educational proficiency of pre-school children. The programme has also resulted in a low dropout rate and high retention rate in primary grades.

The ICDS programme has taken evaluation of its components as an integral part of the programme from the very beginning. Two major evaluations were conducted by the Programme Evaluation Organization of Planning Commission in 1978 and 1982. UNICEF supported an independent assessment of the Programme in 1983. The National Institute of Public Co-operation and Child Development conducted a major national study later in 1992. Kaul (1993) reports that in addition to these, numerous external evaluations—"about 300 have been conducted either by NGOs or by the Universities" (p. 244).

On the basis of the findings of the various evaluations conducted so far by different organizations and individuals, NIPCCD (1992) concludes:

"A review of the various studies indicates that ICDS has a positive impact on beneficiaries and has the potential of enhancing the child survival rate. Definite improvement has been reported on major indicators of health and nutrition like Infant Mortality Rate (IMR), nutritional status, Morbidity Pattern, immunization coverage and utilization of health services. In primary schools, children from ICDS areas were having better competencies on language, cognitive and conceptual development, and behaviour parameters as compared to their counterparts in non-ICDS areas. Improvement in enrollment and scholastic performance further indicated a positive impact of preschool education components of ICDS" (p. 5).

Achievements of the Programme

As mentioned earlier, a nationwide evaluation of ICDS programme was conducted by NIPCCD in the year 1990-92. The sample selected for the study covered about 9 per cent of the total ICDS projects spread over 25 States and one Union Territory. This is one of the most comprehensive evaluations of ICDS at the national level.

Some of the major achievements of the programme as revealed by the national evaluation conducted in 1992 are:

- *Positive Impact on Health and Nutritional Status*: Higher percentage of babies had low birth weight in non-ICDS as compared to ICDS areas, which is a distinctive achievement of ICDS inputs. Nutritional status of children in ICDS areas was better than that of children in non-ICDS areas. Higher percentage of mothers in ICDS areas got their children aged 0-3 years medically examined as against their counterparts in non-ICDS area. The coverage of children for immunization was higher in ICDS areas than non-ICDS areas. A higher percentage of expectant mothers in ICDS areas received tetanus vaccine as against their counterparts in non-ICDS areas such services were utilized only by 30 per cent of expectant mothers.

➢ *Improved Infant Mortality Rate*: Infant Mortality Rates (IMR) in ICDS areas were 81.4; 74.0 and 66.6 per 1000 live births for urban and rural areas respectively which were lower than the non-ICDS 86.0 per 1000 live births (national figure) (Development of Women and Child Development, 1994).

➢ *Improved Access to Pre-school Education*: The coverage of children in ICDS areas under pre-school education was higher (about 85%) than the children in non-ICDS areas (23.5%). A large population of children (85%) in primary schools were with pre-school experience in ICDS areas, whereas the population of children with pre-school experience in non-ICDS areas were very low (15%).

➢ *Improved Primary School Enrolment and Retention Rates:* The preschool education component of ICDS had raised school enrolment and retention rate and reduced the drop-out rate in the elementary school, which was a very important achievement of the programme.

Constraints of the Programme

Some of the major constraints of the programme as revealed by the national study of 1992 are:

➢ *Poor Physical Infrastructure of AW Centres*: Over 80 per cent of Anganwadi centres had no toilet facilities available. About 79 per cent centres had unsatisfactory drainage system. Fifty per cent of centres in tribal areas and 33 per cent in rural and urban projects were being run in *Kutcha* and semi-permanent structures. Only 50 per cent of centres had adequate indoor and outdoor spaces for preschool and play activities.

- *Lack of Community Involvement*: More than 90 per cent of households had not rendered any support for implementation of ICDS services, which was a major drawback of the programme related to community participation. Mahila Mandals were operational only in less than half the number of Anganwadi centres. On the one hand, in most cases ICDS functionaries did not approach community representatives (80%) and were not aware about ways and means by which they could make some contributions to the programme.
- *Limited Time for Early Childhood Education Activities:* Anganwadi Workers devoted only one to two hours a day to early childhood education activities. Most of the time was taken by nutrition and health related activities.
- *Inadequate Supervisory Practices*: On an average, a Supervisor looked after over 30 Anganwadi centres. As a result more than 70 per cent of Supervisors were unable to meet the prescribed schedule of visiting all Anganwadi centres.

Background Information on Nepal

General information about the geographical features, political system, population, economic condition, and educational status of Nepal is presented below:

Geographical Conditions

Nepal is a landlocked country with the Tibetan Autonomous Region of China lying to its North and India lying to its East, South and West. It covers an area of 147,181 square kilometres. The shape of the country is rectangular with an extent of about

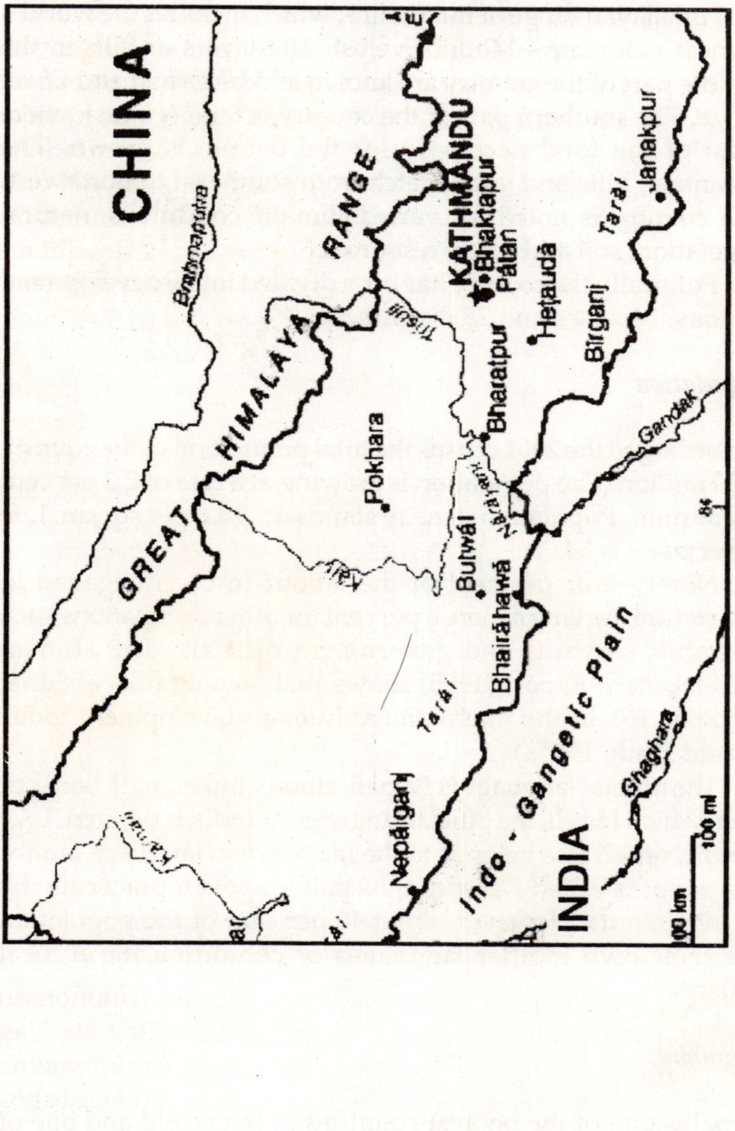

Fig. 5.1: Map of Nepal

885 kilometres. Its breadth from north to south varies from 241 to 145 kilometres with an average of 193 kilometres. The western part of Nepal is wider than the eastern part.

Nepal is known as the Himalayan Kingdom with diverse landmass topography. In the northern part of the country is the Himalayan range of mountains, which includes the world's highest mountain—Mount Everest. The layers of hills in the middle part of the country are known as *Mahabharat* and *Chure* range. The southern part of the country is terai (plains) where most of the food necessary for the people is grown. The mountain, hills and terai stretch from southeast to northwest. The country is noted for varied climatic conditions, natural vegetation, soil and forest resources.

Politically the country has been divided into 5 development regions, 14 zones and 75 districts.

Population

According to the 2001 census the total population of the country is 23 million. The population is growing at a rate of 2.3 per cent per annum. Population density stands at 128.6 per sq. km. Life expectancy is 54.

Ninety-four per cent of the labour force is engaged in agriculture, leaving a mere 6 per cent for other occupations such as public servants and government officials. The Human Development Report (1995) shows that Nepal ranks at Serial Number 151 in the international human development index (World Bank, 1995a).

The official language is Nepali, closely linked with Sanskrit from which Hindi, the official language of India is derived. Like Hindi, Nepali also belongs to the Indo-Aryan language family. The script is called *Devanagri*. Nepali is spoken practically by all inhabitants. However, about 40 per cent of the population use their own mother languages or communicate in local dialects.

Economy

Nepal is one of the poorest countries in the world and one of the least developed nations in South Asia. In Nepal, except for a few professionals, businessmen, and some large farmers, everyone is poor (National Planning Commission/HMG & UNICEF, 1992). The situation of Nepal is characterized by low GNP and relatively high population growth rate (Evans, 1992). The per capita GNP stands at US $ 244 (Central Bureau of Statistics, 2001). About 43 percent of the country's national population is living in absolute poverty (Nepal South Asia Center, 1998) Nepal's social development indicators are among the worst in Asia. Its developmental capacity is limited by low literacy, poor health, inadequate nutrition and persistent poverty (CIDA, 1993).

Nepal is rich in water resources. It has about six thousand big and small rivers. In the field of water potential Nepal holds the second position in the world after Brazil. The country possesses about 2.27 per cent of the world's water resources (Central Bureau of Statistics, 2001). Its estimated hydro-electricity potential is 83 million kilowatts of which 20 to 25 million kilowatts is economically exploitable. However, Nepal has been able to exploit only a fraction of this huge potential of water resource.

Nepal is endowed with various other natural resources such as iron, copper, zinc, silver, slate, marble, limestone, gold, coal, platinum at different parts all over the country. But a number of these minerals are not economically exploitable.

Nepal remains dependent on external financing for as much as 65 per cent of its development budget. The total external debt in 1990 was US $ 1,621 million.

Political System

Nepal as a modern nation came into existence in the later half of the 18th century when the small kingdoms and principalities scattered over the mountains, hills and plains were unified by King Prithvi Narayan Shah the Great, the forefather of the present king. Before the unification of the country by Prithivi Narayan Shah, the country was ruled by different dynasties like Kirats, the Lichhavis and the Mallas in different periods.

In the second half of the British rule in India, the Shah dynasty was over-ruled by the Rana regime for 104 years until 1950 A.D. In 1950, the Rana regime was over-thrown and multi-party democracy was installed and practiced for some years. But King Mahendra, the father of the present King abolished the system and assumed power. He introduced the political system known as Partyless Panchayat System, which lasted for 30 years till 1990. In 1990, Nepal underwent changes in government became responsible to the people. The new popular constitution guarantees basic freedom to the people of Nepal.

Educational Status

The national literacy rate is reported to be 57 per cent. But the female literacy rate is only 44 per cent (Central Bureau of Statistics, 2001). To increase the literacy rate and access to basic education, various programmes such as functional literacy programmes, out-of-school programme for school-age children, special schools, dress and incentives/scholarship programmes for girls etc. have been launched. Primary education has been made free for all children in Nepal since 1975. Textbooks have been provided free of cost to all children in primary grades since 1979. As a result, the net enrolment of primary school children reached 69.4 per cent in 1996. In the field of qualitative improvement the record is very poor. The dropout and repetition rates are high, particularly at the first grade of primary education. It was found that 21 per cent of children drop out and 42 per cent repeat the first grade of primary education. The percentage of trained teachers at the primary level is only 42 per cent. The net enrolment at the secondary level is only 18.2 (MOE, 1998). The Higher Education is available to a very limited number of students.

Status of Pre-School Children in Nepal

The population of children below 6 years of age comprises more than 18 per cent of the total population. Among them about half the children (9.77% of total population) fall under the age group of 3 to 6 years. The present educational status of children in Nepal is low because of the poor social and economic conditions of the country. Nepal is considered as one of the least developed countries in the world.

Most of the people in Nepal live in remote rural areas, which do not even have basic infrastructure like roads, pure drinking water, electricity and health services. As a result, the country has a high infant mortality rate (75 per 1,000). The under-five mortality rate remains at 104 per one thousand live births (UNICEF, 2001). Those who survive also suffer from various ailments, diseases and deformities. The incidence of morbidity is very high and it directly affects the psychosocial and physical development of children. It is estimated that 50 per cent of under-five children suffer from severe or moderate level of malnutrition. Among them, the rate of the proportion of Protein Energy Malnutrition (PEM) is very high. A large number of children suffer from Iodine Deficiency Disorder (IDD) and Iron Deficiency Anaemia. It is no wonder, therefore, that during the critical growing phase, a majority of the children in Nepal suffer from either lack of food or inappropriate feeding, unhygienic state of the physical environment, and lack of basic services including Early Childhood Care and Education (ECCE).

Concerning the status of pre-school children and ECCE in Nepal, the Situation Analysis of Children and Women of Nepal carried out by National Planning Commission, HMG of Nepal & UNICEF, (1992) reveal that.

"By the stage of early childhood, most children in Nepal, by necessity, are being looked after by other children. These siblings, who may be as young as 5 or 6 years old themselves, are the main source of information and the main providers of care to the young child ...Pre-school education is a rarity available only to an extremely small minority of Nepalese children ...The need for an environment which can facilitate the psycho-social development of young children has not yet [been] fully recognized." (pp. 62 & 63).

The entrance to formal schooling, i.e. entrance to grade-I in Nepal begins only from 6 years of age. However, it is estimated that 30-40 per cent of those who attend grade-I are less than 6 years old (Action Plan, 1992, quoted in Evans, W92, p. 13). The children in the age group 3-5 years, either attend school with their elder siblings or the latter also stay at home. This has resulted in phenomenal increase in enrolment comprising under-age children in grade I, which; in turn; accounts for a, high rate of dropout and grade repetition (UNICEF, 1994).

Situation of ECCE in Nepal

History of ECCE in Nepal

The history of organized Early Childhood Care and Education provision in Nepal is not long. It is still new in the Nepalese context. The first Montessori school established in 1950 at Kathmandu, the capital city of the country, is considered as the first ECCE centre in Nepal. The teachers for Montessori School were trained in India. In 1962, some of the teachers were first sent abroad, to Israel, for the training related to ECCE. This remained a single school, which catred to a very limited number of children for many years.

The establishment of Nepal Children's Organization (NCO) in 1962 led to the expansion of ECCE services in an organized manner. This organization has established a Child Care Centre (CCC) in each district of the kingdom. However, as the CCCs established by NCO are located at the district headquarters, they primarily serve the need of the urban or suburban residents and the children of the government officials working at district headquarters.

Opening of pre-school education classes by private schools in the early 70s made ECCE services accessible to a large number of children in the country. Now, even in small cities, one can find privately run pre-school centres by the names of Pre-Primary School, Day Care Centre, Nursery School, Kindergarten School, Child Care Centre, etc. As the privately run schools depend solely on the fees collected from the children enrolled, they cater only to the needs of rich families. Moreover, these schools are confined to urban areas.

The implementation of rural development projects in the mid-80s such as Small Farmers Development Project (SFDP) and Production Credit for Rural Women (PCRW) Projects and their focus on the establishment of CCCs, basically to free the mothers for their involvement in income generating activities, have helped in making available ECCE services to the children living in rural areas albeit to a limited extent. Similarly, since the late 80s and early 90s many international NGOs like Action Aid, Save the Children/US, Save the Children, Norway, Plan International, and the government organizations like Basic and Primary Education Project (BPEP) have been providing ECCE services in the country.

National Plans and Policies on ECCE

Although the reports of Nepal National Education Planning Commission 1956 (2012 B.S.) and All-round National Education Committee 1962 (2018 B.S.) had stressed on the importance of ECCE, the programmes for the education and development of pre-school children did not find a place in the national plans until the Seventh Five Year Plan (National-Education Commission, HMG of Nepal, 1994). Only in the Seventh Five Year Plan (1985-90) was a provision made for the expansion of pre-primary education basically to help reduce the high repetition rate in grade one. Since then the government has included ECCE in the National Five Year Plans, Ten Year National Programme of Action (POA) for Children and Development (1992), Education for All (EFA): Plan of Action (1992-2000), and Basic and Primary Education (BPE) Master Plan (1997-2002). A review of these plans revealed the current policies on ECCE as follows:

Realization of the Need for ECCE

The plans and policies developed so far have indicated the need for expanding ECCE for child development. In the Ninth Plan (1997-2002), the government laid emphasis on implementing appropriate early childhood development programmes for children below five years of age including the children living in remote and rural areas. The Ninth Plan recognized children as the future backbone of the country:

- Mobilize non-governmental, social organizations and local government for implementing ECCE programmes.

Beginning from the Seventh Plan to the Ninth Plan emphasis is being placed on mobilizing families and local communities to make available the resources required for running ECCE programmes. From the Seventh Plan (1985-90) to the Ninth Plan (1997-2002), the government's role is being limited to providing technical assistance, such as EDC teacher's training and educational materials to the centres. Stress is being placed on mobilizing NGOs, and local communities to make available the resources required for running the ECD centers. The POA for Children and Development has stressed securing resources from donor agencies for the cause of child development and mobilizing international and national NGOs and voluntary organizations. The Local Self-government Act of the Government, promulgated in 1999, has given the rights to the local governments—Village Development Committees in the case of rural areas and municipalities in the case of urban localities—to establish pre-primary school centres with their own resources, and issue permissions to establish, implement and organize pre-school centres.

Encouraged Launching Parental Education Programme

In the Ninth Plan the non-governmental and social organizations are encouraged to launch parental education programmes. The BPE Master Plan has stated one of its goals as to create awareness among parents of the need for providing facilities to help children develop their innate capabilities before entering primary schools.

Use of communication media, such as radio and television for initiating and expanding ECCE services

Making people aware about the need for ECCE has been stressed in the plan developed so far. In the Education for All: Plan of Action, one of the strategies suggested for expanding ECCE services was the dissemination of information about the importance of pre-primary education through mass media. In the Ninth Plan it is stated that the communication media, such as radio and television will be encouraged to broadcast child-related programmes for the personality and psychosocial development of children. The BPE Master Plan has stressed the need for using mass media to convey the message of ECCE to the parents in rural and remote areas.

Emphasis on Adopting a Community-based Approach

In order to secure community support and sustainability of the programme as well as for efficient implementation of ECCE programmes, emphasis is being placed on encouraging and facilitating the growth of community-based early child care and education programmes. The POA for children and development and the Ninth Plan have specifically pointed out that the early child development programmes will be implemented by adopting a community-based approach.

Importance of co-ordination among the relevant organizations and programmes for child development.

Importance of co-ordination among the various relevant organizations has been pointed out since the very beginning of the implementation of the Seventh Plan. The Ninth Plan has pointed out the importance of co-ordination, monitoring and evaluation of child development programmes run by the Government, national and international non-governmental organizsations and other organizations. In order to co-ordinate the activities of various organizations the BPE Master Plan has recommended the formation of various committees. The Plan has suggested the formation of a national committee on ECCE involving members of the National Planning Commission and the relevant Ministries. The POA for the Children and Development pointed out the importance of a unified strategy for child development. It recognized that "fragmented and isolated efforts by different sectors and agencies are costly and therefore, a co-ordinated and integrated approach with cross-sectional linkages is essential" [National Planning Commission (NPC), HMG of Nepal, 1992, (p. 7)].

Low-cost Pre-primary Education

The EFA: Plan of Action has advocated for low-cost pre-primary education. It has underlined the use of locally available low-cost materials. It has also emphasized to recruit teachers/facilitators from the local community and provide preference for women facilitators in the recruitment process. Moreover, it has also emphasized to encourage play-way activities in the pre-primary education centres.

Situation of ECCE in Nepal

In Nepal various forms of ECCE programmes are being implemented by the government, national and international non-governmental organizations and private individuals. Almost all the programmes run are targeted to the children aged 3 to 5. ECCE programmes have not yet laid adequate emphasis on the provision of child development services to children below 3 years of age. Services for the development of children from conception to three years of age are, to a larger extent, being looked after by the Ministry of Health through its maternal and child health programmes. However, the services provided by the Ministry of Health lack the early stimulation components required for psychosocial and emotional development of children.

In the present organizational structure, although early childhood education is being undertaken by the Ministry of Education and Sports, the care and education of children aged 3 to 5 years are not formally included in any ministry. Management of ECCE does not fall under the formal structure of any of the ministries of the government programme; the government has not allocated funds for ECCE in its regular budget.

The entrance to the formal schooling, i.e. entrance to grade-I, in Nepal begins only from 6 years of age. However, it is estimated that 30-40 per cent of those who attend grade-I are less than 6 years old. To cope with this problem the Ministry of Education under its multi-donor project Basic and Primary Education, has launched pre-school education programme. There is a plan to establish 5,700 pre-primary schools under this project during the Ninth Plan period.

INGOs, such as Save the Children/US, Save the Children Norway (Redd Barna), PLAN International, have been running ECCD programmes in partnership with local NGOs. However, the number of children covered by these organizations are very limited. Most of the programmes run are not being sustained.

Most of the ECCE programmes run by the government and non-governmental organizations and almost all the ECCE programmes run by the private organizations resort to teaching of three Rs with no health and nutrition inputs.

According to ERA Assessment Committee, Ministry of Education, some kind of organized ECCE services are available to about 8 per cent of children aged 3 to 5 years.

The programmes being run lack an integrated approach for the holistic development of children. Developing a comprehensive ECCE programme that caters to the needs of a child from conception to below 6 years of age and making ECCE accessible to children living in rural and disadvantaged situations are the two major challenges in Nepal.

Most of the ECCE programmes especially run by private organizations in Nepal are confined to urban areas. As ECCE Centres run by private Organizations charge high fees to the children, the services provided by private organizations are not accessible to children belonging to poor economic background living in rural and disadvantaged situations. Most of the people in Nepal are living in remote rural areas, which do not have basic facilities like roads, pure drinking water, electricity and health services.

In the communities where there is no access to organized ECCE services, in extended types of families, the children are usually taken care of by the family as a whole. At the age of four onward, children are either left on their own or placed under the care of an older sibling. In a nuclear family, where there is no older sibling, cases of harsh examples of "Child-care" are pervasive. For example, infants are bound to a pole or pillar with a piece of rope so that she would be prevented from reaching harmful objects while the parents are away.

Lessons Nepal could Learn from the Indian Experience

Nepal's social, cultural and topography resembles, that of India in many respects. The living standards of people, especially those of the marginalized groups of both the countries are very much the same. There are many common issues of development of the poor people. The situations of young children of both the countries are also not very different. It is, against this background that Nepal should learn important lessons from the Indian experiences in expanding Early Childhood Care and Education services in Nepal. Learning from the Indian experiences can save the meagre resources available for early childhood development in Nepal keeping in view the situation of young children and ECCE in Nepal. As described above, Nepal should learn lessons from Indian experiences for improving its ECCE services. On the basis of the critical analysis of the successful strategies and achievements as well as the constrains or bottlenecks of the programme, Nepal can learn the following lessons:

Have a Strong Political Commitment

For implementing a large-scale national programme targeted to the children living in rural and disadvantaged situations it is important for the government to have a strong political commitment. In order to provide proper care and education to the children, especially those living in the rural and disadvantaged situations, the ICDS programme is an ideal model. There is an urgent need for designing and implementing a comprehensive integrated child development programme in Nepal on the lines of ICDS—Political will and commitment is a must for developing a comprehensive programme for the all-round development of children living in rural and disadvantaged situations. The government in Nepal should learn from Indian experiences and develop Integrated Child Development Services scheme for the development of children in Nepal. For this, the government should first of all show a strong will and develop a political commitment for implementing such a large-scale integrated child development programme.

Involve Related Ministries, Departments and Organizations and Co-ordinate their Activities

For providing integrated services to the children and women on a large scale, it is important to involve related ministries, departments and organizations. The activities of the organizations working in the field of ECCE at various levels need to be co-ordinated well. To ensure the effective co-ordination and co-operation among various ministries, departments, organizations and local bodies, as in ICDS programme, Co-ordination Committees need to be formed at different levels. This will increase efficiency and help eliminate duplication of work. Inter-organizational co-ordination is highly important from the point of view of the holistic development of children. Co-ordination of the organizations related to health, nutrition, education and rural development would help achieve synergy for better results. Such co-ordination ensures cost effectiveness and high efficiency in the services delivered.

By establishing a functional co-ordination among the relevant departments and organizations, health and nutrition related personnel working in the ministry of health, and other relevant ministries and departments need to be involved in providing health and nutrition related services to children, and expectant and lactating mothers covered by the ECCE programmes. Similarly, in providing training to the ECCE functionaries the expertise and facilities of established institutes need to be utilized. The Ministry of Health with its departments and many NGOs and INGOs are involved in the delivery of health services in Nepal. Similarly, many organizations are involved in the delivery of nutrition education and food supply activities. ECCE programmes should strive to procure health and nutrition services of the concerned organizations for their children: Inter-organizational co-ordination can support inter-related activities and make delivery of services cost effective.

Involve Concerned Ministries, Departments and Organizations from the very Beginning of Programme Development

The history of ICDS programme shows that the concerned ministries, departments and organizations were involved in the development of ICDS programme from the very beginning. Even before the development of ICDS scheme, inter-ministry meetings were held and eight inter-ministerial teams were formed by the Planning Commission to conduct a quick survey on the feasibility of implementing integrated childcare services. In Nepal, the National Planning Commission should take the initiative and involve relevant ministries in the development of an integrated early childcare and education programme for children especially those living in rural and disadvantaged situations in Nepal.

Invest on ECCE

One of the reasons why ECCE has not been universally accessible is finance. Finance plays a vital role in providing any kind of service, ECE being no exception. The existing state of shifting financial responsibilities for ECE to the local community and parents cannot improve quality of ECE and its expansion in Nepal. Two important things need to be considered while managing financial resources for ECE. First, it should not be forgotten that proper management could help minimize the wastage. Secondly, investment in early education can bring high return in the future. Expenditure on ECE should be regarded as an investment for human resources development rather than in an unproductive area. It is important to recognize that the human resource development is the surest key to national development. The foundation for this development is laid before the child enters the primary school. Keeping in view the long-term possible impact of the effective ECCE programme, the government needs to make budgetary provisions for the welfare of children below

6 years of age. In order to provide Early Childhood Care and Education services to the children living in rural urban slums and disadvantaged situations, it is important that the government should allocate funds in its national budget. Funds need to be mobilized from international donor agencies in order to facilitate the implementation of ECCE programme. Efforts need to be made for mobilizing local, physical and financial resource for providing ECCE services. The investment on ECCE should be considered as investment in human resource development. It is important to recognize that investing in early years of life can bring high return in later life.

Adopt a Positive Discriminatory Approach

The ICDS programme is targeted at the poor and disadvantaged children living in rural urban slums. The programme exclusively dispenses services to targeted population. Many research studies have shown that ECCE services can have a profound effect on the survival, growth and development of children living in vulnerable situations as compared to the children in better off families. So, in line with the ICDS scheme, a positively discriminatory approach has to be adopted for the children living in rural and disadvantaged situation in Nepal. Instead of making ECCE free for all it should be made free only for those who are poor. The national budget should be utilized for making up the deficiency of funds. For the children living in urban areas and belonging to rich families, the private sector needs to be encouraged. The programme targeted at the poor and disadvantaged children should dispense services exclusively to the targeted population.

Adopt an Integrated Approach for Holistic Development of Children

One of the important lessons that other developing countries with low GDP could learn from Indian experience in implementing child development programme is the integrated approach for holistic development of children. For the holistic development of the child the ICDS scheme has integrated the programme of health, nutrition and early childhood education, and extended its services to the children in the age group of 5 to 6 years and their mothers. Its package of services includes supplementary nutrition, immunizations, health check up, referral services, non-formal pre-school education, and nutrition and health education for children below six years and to pregnant and nursing mothers.

In an integrated ECCE programme that caters to the health, nutrition and educational needs of the children it is important to give appropriate emphasis to each component. It is necessary that there be no overlap or over-emphasis on one component over the others. The ICDS programme is criticized for putting heavy emphasis on nutrition programme. The programme is even, to some extent, known as nutrition programme. From the ICDS experience it is important to ensure that the supplementary nutrition programme does not dominate the other activities of the ECCE programme in Nepal.

Develop Basic Physical Infrastructure

The basic physical infrastructure in most of the ICDS centres is considered as poor. The physical infrastructure required for running a child care centre includes building or a room or indoor space, furniture, drinking water facilities; toilet and outdoors space or play ground. For the effective implementation of ECCE programme it is important to develop a basic physical infrastructure. Renting a room for the center could be a temporary measure but for making ECCE centre a permanent institution it is important to construct its own building. The physical infrastructure of the ECCE centres needs to be improved on a priority basis. It is important to secure public land and building for ECCE programme wherever such facilities are available. Local resources available need to be mobilized in order to make the necessary physical infrastructure available for the ECCE programme.

Follow the Basic Principles of ECCE

It is important to ensure that the ECCE programmes follow the basic principles of ECCE. Emphasis on formal teaching, rote memorization and teaching of the three Rs should be discouraged. For this it is necessary to take three measures: (a) creating awareness in the people through mass media about the harm that formal teaching and the teaching of three Rs does to the development of children at the early age, (b) providing adequate training to the child care workers on proper care and education of young children, and (c) formulation of code of conduct and laws forbidding the activities detrimental to the pre-school aged children, and encouraging child-centred play-way activities at ECCE centers.

Involve Parents and Community People in the Management of ECCE Programme

The concept of users groups is the best way of turning the feeling of theirs into ours. For the effective implementation and sustainability of the programme, it is important that parents be maximally involved. Formation of "mothers group", as in ICDS programme, and activating the group can be a viable strategy for involving parents in ECCE programme. The poor parents contribute by undertaking voluntary work such as keeping the centre and children clean, feeding children, helping in the production of children's learning materials at the ECCE centre.

People from local community such as social workers, school teachers, political leaders, and officials can support the programme by making available their expertise and by devoting time for mobilizing resources and managing and monitoring the ECCE programmes: Formation of ECCE centre management committees comprising people from different walks of life and securing their voluntary services can be a good strategy for involving local community in ECCE programme.

REFERENCES

Canadian International Development Agency (CIDA) (1993). CIDA programme in Asia. Nepal: Canadian International Development Agency (CIDA) Asia Branch.

Central Bureau of Statistics. (2001). *Statistical Yearbook of Nepal, Kathmandu*: Author.

Department of Women and Child Development, Government of India. (1994). *Annual Report, Part IV*, 1993-94. New Delhi: Author.

Evans, J. L. (1992). Nepal: from entry point to consolidation. An assessment of early childhood provision in Nepal with recommendations for UNICEF's involvement. Report of a Consultancy, submitted to UNICEF/Nepal. Unpublished research report.

Heaver, R. A. and Hunt, J. M. (1995). *Improving early childhood development: An integrated programme for the Philippines*. Washington, D. C.: The World Bank.

Kaul, V. (1993). *Integrated Child Development Services in India. In childhood* Vol. I, 1993. Denmark, Munksaard.

Ministry of Education, HMG of Nepal (MOE). (1998). *Educational statistics of Nepal* (1996). Kathmandu: Planning Division, Ministry of Education.

Ministry of Human Resource Development, Government of India. (1995). *Annual Report, 1995*. New Delhi: Author.

Murlidharan, R., and Kaul, V. (1993). Early childhood care and education: Current status and problems. In Saraswathi, T. S. and Kaur, B. (eds.). *Human development and family studies in India* (An agenda for research and policy). New Delhi: Sage Publication India Pvt. Ltd.

Myres, R. G. (1993). Foreword. In Saraswathi, T.S. & Kaur, (eds.) *Human development and family studies in India. An Agenda for Research and Policy* New Delhi: Sage Publications.

National Education Commission (NEC), HMG of Nepal. (1994). *Rastriya Shiksha Aayog ko Pratibedan* (Report of National Education Commission 1994; (in Nepali language). Kathmandu: National Education Commission (NEC).

National Institute of Public Co-operation and Child Development (NIPCCD). (1992). *National evaluation of integrated child development services*. New Delhi: Author.

National Planning Commission (NPC), HMG of Nepal. (1992). *National programme of action for children and development for 1990s*. Kathmandu: Author.

National Planning Commission, HMG of Nepal. (1985). *The Ninth Plan 1997-2002*. Kathmandu, Nepal: Author.

National Planning Commission, HMG of Nepal. (1985). *The Seventh Plan 1985-90*. Kathmandu, Nepal: Author.

Nepal South Asia Centre. (1998). *Nepal Human Development Report 1998*. Kathmandu: Author.

Sadka, N. L. (1984). *Integrated Child Development Services* (ICDS). New Delhi: UNICEF, Regional Office for South Central Asia.

United Nations Children's Fund (UNICEF). (1994). *ECE Programme in Nepal: Its status and resources*. Unpublished document. Kathmandu: Author.

United Nations Children's Fund (UNICEF). (2001). *The State of the World's Children 2001*. New York: Author.

World Bank. (1995a). *World Development Report 1995*. Washington D.C. Oxford University Press.

World Bank. (1996). *Early Childhood Development: Investing in the Future*. Washington, D.C.: Author.

6

Asian and Euro-American Parents' Ethnotheories of Play and Learning: Effects on Pre-school Children's Home Routines and School Behaviour

PARMINDER PARMAR, SARA HARKNESS
and CHARLES M. SUPER

Play is a universal activity among young children, but its nature varies across cultures in response to specific constraints and differential degrees of encouragement (Farver, 1999; Gaskins, 1999; Harkness & Super, 1986; Schwartzman, 1978). Among the US middle-class, the importance of play for the development of young children has become part of conventional folk wisdom (Lightfoot & Valsiner, 1992), and this perspective corresponds at least in part to major developmental theories such as those of Piaget (1962) and Vygotsky (1976, 1978). For the American middle class, play—and the toys that are manufactured to support play are generally thought to be necessary for the stimulation of cognitive and social development, crucial for success in school and in later life.

Parents' cultural belief systems, or "parental ethnotheories," have been shown to influence the organization of children's environments of learning and development in many different societies (Harkness and Super, 1992, 1999; Roopnarine, Johnson, & Hooper, 1994; Roopnarine, Lasker, Sacks, and Stores, 1998). Cultural beliefs about play in children's development vary widely, suggesting that the current U.S. emphasis on the importance of play is far from universal. For example, Harkness and Super (1986) found that Kipsigis mothers in a rural African community did not consider themselves appropriate playmates for their children, and the amount of time that children spent in assigned work settings (as opposed to play) rose to fifty per cent by the age of six years. In this community, both, work and play were intertwined into a virtually seamless fabric of daily life. Rogoff, Mistry, Göncü, & Mosier (1993) report that Mayan mothers did not consider play to be important for the development of their children. Research with North American, Mexican, and Indonesian toddlers has also shown that American mothers, who valued play for its educational and cognitive benefits, were more likely to join their children's play activities and to provide props and suggestions that encourage expression in pretend play. On the other hand, Mexican and Indonesian mothers, who viewed children's play as just for amusement, did not play with their children or facilitate play (Farver & Howes, 1993; Farver & Wimbarti, 1995). Similarly, Farver, Kim and Lee (1995) found that in comparison with Anglo-American parents, Korean American parents believed academics to be more important than play, and they engaged in less pretend play with their children.

Asian parents' educational practices with school-age children have been the focus of several major investigations in recent years (Stevenson, Lee, Chen, & Lummis, 1990; Stevenson, Lee, Chen, & Stigler, 1990). Chen and Stevenson (1995) found that Chinese students were assigned more homework and spent more time on homework than Japanese children, who in turn were assigned more and spent more time on homework than U.S. children. Likewise, Huntsinger, Jose, Liaw, and Ching (1997) found that Chinese American parents taught their preschool children in more formal ways, were more directive, and structured their children's use of time to a greater degree than did Euro-American parents. These practices support Asian parents' belief in the importance of a good education for success in life (Chao, 1996, 2000). However, there has been little research that explores how these beliefs relate to the ways that parents think about their children's development or how parents organize children's environments of daily life at home, especially for pre-school children's play and learning. Cross-cultural studies suggest that the organization of the home environment is generally consonant with parental beliefs, but the directive force of parental ethnotheories is not always evident in such studies because many other factors in the broader environment work together in shaping children's environments of daily life (Harkness & Super, 1996; Whiting & Edwards, 1988).

The cultural beliefs and practices of Asian parents of preschoolers are of particular interest because of wide differences in children's academic performance that have been observed both, cross-culturally and within the U.S., with Asian children tending to excel, especially in mathematics and sciences (Chen & Stevenson, 1995; Stevenson et al., 1990). In the U.S. context, Asian children have presented a different kind of challenge from most other immigrant groups. On the one hand, high-achieving Asian children offer possible models for how American parents and schools could be more effective in educating children. On the other hand, many parents and teachers wonder whether Asian children may be subjected to too much pressure to do well in school, at the expense of other developmentally appropriate activities. The American concept of play as an important developmental context in early childhood may be incompatible with different cultural beliefs about good parenting. In addition, the prototypical American pre-school context itself, with its usual emphasis on play, may conflict with expectations of Asian parents and may present difficulties in adaptation to children who may not have had the same kinds of practice in play at home.

The present research, thus, was designed to explore the "developmental niches" of Asian and American pre-school children (Super & Harkness, 1999), in which play and learning activities might differ in accordance with differing parental ethnotheories. Specifically, we expected that Asian parents would place more emphasis on their roles as teachers than as playmates, and that these ideas would be reflected in the ways that parents in each cultural group organized home environments and daily routines for their pre-school children. We also investigated whether cultural differences in children's developmental niches at home might be reflected in differences in their behaviour in pre-school as observed by their teachers. Such differences, we imagined, might ultimately influence both, the child's adaptation to pre-school and the nature of parent-teacher relationships across these two ethnic groups.

Methods

Participants

Participants in this study were Euro-American and Asian parents of children attending three preschools in northeast Connecticut, and the children's teachers. The 24 target children in each cultural sample ranged in age from 3 to 6 years, with an equal number of boys and girls in each. In order to examine child age effects on patterns of parental response, the samples were divided into younger (36 to 54 months) and older (55 to 72 months) for some analyses. In both cultural samples, there were 13 children in the younger group and 11 in the older. Mothers and fathers in both the Euro-American and Asian samples were highly educated (mean years = 17 except Asian fathers =18), and they held professional jobs. Hollingshead (1975) scores for the two groups were essentially equivalent (Euro-American = 56 vs. Asian = 55). Fathers in the two samples were similar in age (Euro-American = 38 years vs. Asian = 37 years), but there was a small difference between the two groups of mothers (36 vs. 33, respectively). The mean number of children was not significantly different between the groups (Euro-American = 1.7 vs. Asian = 1.5), nor was household size (3.7 Euro-American vs. 3.5 Asian), age of the target child (56 vs. 57 months respectively), number of hours per week that the child attended pre-school (30 for the Euro-American children and 31 for Asians) or living accommodations (54 per cent of the Euro-American families lived in private houses rather than apartments, as did 42 per cent of the Asian families).

The Asian children were from China (6), Korea (4), Pakistan (4), Nepal (4), and India (6). Their parents had been living in the U.S. for up to 10 years, with an average of 6 years' residence. They were new immigrants or were in the process of acquiring permanent resident status; 83 per cent of the Asian children had been born in their country of origin. Although some regional differences were evident among the Asian sub-groups (for example, the Nepalese and Pakistani parents appeared least assimilated to US customs, and the Korean parents reported doing more art work and music with their children), there are no significant sub-group differences on the Hollingshead scale.

Measures

In addition to the demographic background questionnaire, two questionnaires were used to gather information about the parents' beliefs and practices related to play and learning. The parents also filled out a daily activities checklist about their child for a week, and they were interviewed in a semi-structured format about their beliefs and practices related to children's play and learning. The parent interviews were conducted in the families' homes, which offered the opportunity to take note of how the living space was organized for children's play and learning. All measures were collected within a four-week period for each family. Finally, the children's teachers also filled out a questionnaire concerning the child's behaviour in the classroom, and the teachers were interviewed about their perceptions of the study children.

The Education Attitude Scale (EAS) by Rescorla (1991) was used to measure parents' expectations and values related to their child's development during the preschool years. The EAS examines attitudes about achievement and performance in three skill areas (academic skills, athletic skills, and artistic/musical skills), and in two social areas (peer relations and compliance). The scale includes 32 statements such as "It's important for my preschooler to learn to be good at recognizing letters," "It's important to me that my preschooler is good at playing with other kids," and "I should work at helping my preschooler learn how to get along with other kids," to be rated on a six-point Likert scale from "strongly agree" to "strongly disagree".

The Preschool Play and Learning Questionnaire (PPLQ) was developed for this study in order to measure parents' beliefs about the importance of play, learning, and their own role in early development. The initial draft included 25 items such as "Play should be just for fun," "Young children learn social skills through play," "Preschoolers should have more books than toys," "Parents should only play with their preschoolers when children ask them to do so," to be rated on a six-point Likert scale from "strongly agree" to "strongly disagree". Ultimately, 13 of these items were retained in three scales that worked equivalently in the two samples, as described below.

The Parental Beliefs Interview was conducted with both parents together. This interview, developed for the present research, uses eight open-ended questions to explore parents' beliefs about the importance of play, how play contributes to development and learning in preschool children, how parents structure the home for play and learning, and parents' expectations regarding preschool or day care. The interview was conducted by the first author, and took about 30 to 45 minutes to complete. Parents' responses were recorded verbatim. As part of the interview home visit, the investigator also observed the physical environment in the home and noted the allocation of space for children's activities, as well as the number and types of toys available to the child.

The Daily Activities Checklist, developed for the present research, was used to assess the ecology of daily life for the study children. Parents kept this checklist for a week, recording the activities related to play and learning that their preschool children were involved in at home each day. For each activity checked, parents noted who was with the child, where the activity took place, and how long the activity lasted.

In order to assess how differences in home experience might influence the children's behaviour in pre-school, teachers were asked to fill out the Child's Behaviour Inventory of Playfulness.

This questionnaire, developed by Rogers, Impara, Farry, Harris, Meeks, Semanic-Lauth, and Reynolds (1998), is a trait-rating instrument suitable for use by parents and teachers. The inventory consists of 28 items using a 5 point Likert scale for rating children's play behaviour from "very uncharacteristic" to "very characteristic". Of the two sub-scales in this instrument, only the one concerning play was used. This sub-scale includes questions like "Child invents new games," "Child pretends a lot," "Child is imaginative," and "Child finds unusual way to use toys/objects."

Finally, the children's teachers provided qualitative information through a brief open-ended interview about their observations of the children in school and on cultural differences between Asian and Euro-American preschoolers in general.

In summary, the measures used for the present study were designed to assess parental ethnotheories about play and learning, their instantiation in practices at home, and effects on children's behaviour at pre-school. Our methods for studying parental ethnotheories and practices included both, structured instruments—questionnaires and forms for noting daily activities, and semi-structured interviews that could be analyzed both, qualitatively and quantitatively. Through use of multiple methods, we were able to identify and analyze particular patterns of similarity and difference in the two cultural groups, as well as in relation to age and gender. This approach has long been a hallmark of interdisciplinary research in culture and human development (Harkness, Hughes, Muller & Super, in press) and it has recently received increasing attention among psychologists who seek to understand development in context (Wachs & Friedman, 1999).

Results

Parents' cultural beliefs about play and learning were assessed through two questionnaires (the Education Attitude Scale and the Preschool Play and Learning Questionnaire) as well as the parent interview. The results of these three measures are consistent with our expectations of cultural differences between the Asian and Euro-American parents, and they also suggest some ways in which culture interacts with child, age and sex to yield distinctive patterns in each group.

Education Attitude Scale (EAS)

The Asian and Euro-American parents differed in their attitudes about children's learning and development, as measured by the Education Attitude Scale. A three-way MANOVA (Culture × Sex × Age) revealed a significant main effect of Culture (F [5,86] = 21.0, p < .001) and a significant interaction effect for Culture × Sex × Age (F[1,86] = 3.0, p < .05). As shown in Table 6.1, univariate ANOVAs on each of the five sub-scales indicate that the effect of Culture is significant for Academics and for Arts, with the Asian parents more strongly endorsing the importance of learning in both these areas. In the third skill area, Athletics, the Asian and Euro-American parents did not differ significantly. Within the two social areas, the Euro-American parents scored significantly higher on the Compliance scale, indicating that they expected more compliance from their children than the Asian parents did.

The three-way interaction appeared only for the Social Skills sub-scale: the Asian parents gave more importance to social skills for their sons than for their daughters at the younger age, but the trend was reversed for the older children. In contrast, the Euro-American parents placed more importance on social qualities for their sons in both age groups.

Table 6.1: Parental Ratings* on Education Attitude Scale (EAS)

Sub-scale	*Euro-American mean and S.D.*	*Asian mean and S.D.*	*p of difference*
Academic	4.13 (.72)	4.77 (.79)	.001
Art	3.64 (.59)	4.47 (.92)	.001
Athletics	3.69 (.66)	4.21 (.77)	n.s.
Compliance	4.72 (.50)	4.28 (.51)	.001
Social	5.36 (.71)	5.22 (.64)	n.s.

* Rating scale goes from 1 to 6 (very important)

Preschool Play and Learning Questionnaire

Visual inspection of the correlations among the 25 original items in the initial draft questionnaire revealed three small clusters of variables that corresponded in meaning and had the same patterns of intercorrelations within each of the two cultural groups. Calculations of reliability confirmed this observation, as shown in Table 6.2. The first cluster, related to the importance of play for development, included five statements endorsing the importance of play for cognitive development, social skills, creativity, and learning. The second cluster, focusing on the importance of early academics for development, included items regarding provision of structured time, practice, and educational toys. The third cluster grouped together items related to the role of parents in children's play, including bedtime reading, playing with children, and providing a play corner for children. Scales were derived from these clusters by finding the mean value of parental ratings for each. A three-way (Culture × Sex × Age) MANOVA on the three scales yielded a main effect for Culture ($F[3,86] = 13.76$, $p < .001$). Univariate ANOVAs, as shown in Table 6.2, indicate that the Euro-American parents placed greater importance on play than did the Asian parents, and they also stressed more their own role in children's play, as partners and as a resource to their children.

Table 6.2: Parental Ratings* on the Preschool Play and Learning Questionnaire

Sub-scale	*Euro- Am. alpha*	*Euro-Am. Mean and S.D.*	*Asian alpha*	*Asian mean and S.D.*	*p of difference*
Importance of Play in development	.69	6.22 (.44)	.65	5.75 (.63)	<.001
Importance of Early academics in development	.74	4.46 (.96)	.65	5.15 (.87)	<.001
Importance of role of parents	.65	6.08 (.60)	.47	5.66 (.64)	<.001

* Rating scale goes from 1 to 7 (very important)

In contrast, the Asian parents placed greater emphasis on the Importance of Early Academics. There was also an Age effect for this scale ($p = .03$), indicating that parents in both cultural groups saw early academic progress to be more important for the older age group.

Parental Beliefs Interview

Two questions from the parental interviews were selected for the present analyses: What is the importance of play for children's development, and what is most important for development during the pre-school years? Parents' responses to these questions were coded for the occurrence of spontaneously expressed ideas as they fell into several inductively derived categories, and the frequencies of occurrence were then tabulated. For these analyses, we assume that the frequency of mentioning a particular idea or theme reflects its salience or importance for the parents.

Regarding the importance of play for children's development, parents' responses fell easily into five categories: Its importance for Development in general; for Physical development; for Cognitive development; for Social development; and for Individual development. A three-way MANOVA (Culture × Sex × Age) was carried out on the frequency of mentions for each of the five categories, yielding a significant main effect only for Culture ($F [5,36] = 5.38$, $p < .001$). Subsequent univariate analyses showed that the Euro-American parents mentioned significantly more than the Asian parents that play is important for development in general, and specifically for children's cognitive development and development as an individual. On the other hand, the Asian parents emphasized significantly more often the importance of play for physical and social development (see Table 6.3).

These cultural differences are illustrated by two typical responses, the first by a Euro-American parent: "We provide an environment that gives our children opportunities to learn, but we do not 'instruct' our children at home. Play itself develops cognitive and social skills. When our children express a desire to explore topics more in depth, we do so; we wait for our children to initiate. We strive to stimulate a life-long interest and love for learning in our children for their own sakes, rather than to satisfy our need for validation by trying to create child geniuses." In contrast, an Asian parent explained that play "is important, very important for physical development. It promotes circulation and respiration, makes [children] stronger. They learn how to get along with other kids and this prepares them for the future. It helps them to share, respect, and cooperate with others."

Table 6.3: Group Differences in Parent Responses on Interview

Parent Responses	*Euro-American Mean*	*Asian Mean*	*p of difference*
Play important for General Development	3.91	2.58	<.001
Play important for Physical Development	0.66	2.12	<.05
Play important for Cognitive Development	1.79	1.33	<.001
Play important for Social Development	1.83	2.04	<.001
Play important for Individual Development	0.29	0.12	<.001
Importance of Play for Fun, Variety	1.70	0.45	<.001
Importance of Social Skills	2.70	4.58	<.001
Importance of Physical development	0.20	0.33	ns
Importance of Development as Individual	1.66	0.62	<.001
Importance of Head Start on Academics	0.62	1.50	<.001
Importance of Cognitive Development	0.12	0.62	ns
Importance of Parents and Family	0.87	1.20	ns

Related contrasts were evident in parents' responses to the question of what is most important for their children's development during the preschool years. The answers were grouped into seven different themes: The importance of Play, Fun, and a Variety of Toys and Experiences; of Learning Social Skills; of Good Physical Development; of Developing as an Individual; of Getting a Head Start on Academics; of Cognitive Development; and of Parents and Family. As indicated in Table 6.3, the Euro-American parents focused their responses on development of the individual self, while the Asian parents emphasized the importance of getting a head start on academic.

Three-way MANOVA (Culture × Sex × Age) showed a significant effect of Culture ($F [7,34] = 4.67, p < .001$). Univariate

ANOVAs indicated the Euro-American families put significantly greater stress than the Asian families on the importance of play, fun and variety of experiences, and on the importance of developing as an individual. In contrast, the Asian parents more frequently mentioned the importance of learning social skills/qualities and the importance of getting an early start in academic development. There were no significant differences between the two cultural groups in the importance of cognition development, physical play and development, or the role of parents and family in the development of preschool children (see Table 6.1).

Once again, brief quotations can illustrate nicely the differences in beliefs. A Euro-American parent stated, "Most important is sharing and cooperation with kids her age. She should have lots of fun, and she should be able to play independently. This is the time to explore the world and develop her identity. She should be exposed to plenty of different experiences. This is also a time to develop positive self-esteem." In contrast, an Asian parent responded to the same question, "She needs lots of love, and a secure environment. She needs books and exposure to alphabets and numbers. She is ready to learn – the earlier the better. If we spend time educating and making her smart now it will be better for her future. This is a time to explore and manipulate the world, and to get knowledge."

Table 6.4: Group Differences in Observed Parental Practices at Home

Measure	*Euro-American*	*Asian*	*p of difference*
Toys, fewer than 50	1	6	—
Toys, 50 to 100	7	16	—
Toys, 100 to 200	10	1	—
Toys, 200 or more	6	1	<.01
Special place for toys (n of cases)	1	7	.02
Own play room (n of cases)	10	7	.05
Toys for fun/pretend play (n of cases)	18	17	.09
Toys for physical play (n of cases)	1	1	ns
Toys for constructive play (n of cases)	13	18	ns
Toys for educational play (n of cases)	17	23	.02
Toys for art and music (n of cases)	8	11	ns

Observations of the Environment

Parents in both samples were similar in education and employment, and enjoyed similar living accommodations and community context. Therefore, we can assume that the way they organized the physical and social settings of their children's daily lives are a rather direct expression of their cultural beliefs and values – these are the daily practices of parenting (Goodnow, Miller, & Kessel, 1995). A number of differences were observed (see Table 6.4). Although children in both cultural groups had toys to play with, the Asian families provided fewer than the Euro-American families, a quarter of whom had over 200 toys for their pre-schoolers. The Asian families tended to have a special place (box, or portion of a room) for the toys, while the Euro-American families were more likely to have a dedicated "play room" for the child. Children in both groups had a variety of different kinds of toys – for pretend play, physical play, constructive play, for art and music, and for educational play – but only in the latter case was there a significant group difference, with the Asian families having more toys for educational play.

Daily Activities Checklist

Data from the Daily Activities Checklist maintained by parents were analyzed for the amount of time spent each week on different kinds of play and learning activities, the different locations in which these activities took place, and with whom children were doing these activities. The activities were grouped into seven main categories: Play activities; Pre-academic activities (such as learning alphabets and number at home); Watching TV; Household chores; Art and Music; Books at bedtime; and Visiting the library. A three-way (Culture × Sex × Age) MANOVA yielded only a significant effect of Culture (F $[1,47] = 9.88$, $p < .001$); univariate ANOVAs revealed significant differences between the two groups on three of the activities. The Euro-American children spent more time on household chores and reading at bedtime, whereas the Asian children spent more time on pre-academic activities and visiting the library. MANOVA yielded no significant differences in the amounts of time that the Euro-American and Asian children spent on overall play activities (F [1, 47] =.07, p<.79, art (F.07 [1, 47] = .06, p< .79, and music. (F.07 [1, 47] = 3.28, p<.07, or watching TV (F [1, 47] =1.17, p<.28. (Table 6.5).

Table 6.5: Group Differences in Children's Daily Activities at Home

Measure	*Euro-American*	*Asian*	*p of difference*
Play (hrs/wk)	15.96	16.98	ns
Play (hrs/wk)	15.96	16.98	ns
Pre-Academic (hrs/wk)	5.52	8.55	<.001
Watching TV (hrs/wk)	4.12	4.90	ns
Household Chores (hrs/wk)	1.23	0.18	<.001
Art and music	2.88	2.23	ns
Visiting Library (hrs/wk)	0.52	1.22	<.05
Reading books at bedtime (hrs/wk)	4.02	2.85	<.05
Pretend Play (hrs/wk)	3.96	2.57	<.04
Physical Play (hrs/wk)	5.70	5.80	ns
Constructive Play (hrs/wk)	2.24	2.65	ns
Board games (hrs/wk)	0.77	1.15	ns
Social Play (hrs/wk)	2.42	2.61	ns
Organized Sports/Lessons (hrs/wk)	0.94	0.54	ns
Pre-Academic: Letters and numbers (hrs/wk)	0.60	2.03	<.001
Pre-Academic: Early math skills (hrs/wk)	0.11	1.14	<.001
Pre-Academic: Alphabet and number games (hrs/wk)	0.26	1.09	<.001
Pre-Academic: Play/learning on computer (hrs/wk)	0.65	1.56	<.05

However, inspired by ethnographic observations, a more detailed analysis of children's play and learning activities was carried out in order to explore group differences in the *kinds* of play and learning activities involved. Play activity was grouped into six categories: Pretend play, Physical play, Constructive play, Board games, Simple Social play, and Organized play or lessons. Univariate analyses (Culture × Sex × Age) of each type revealed a significant difference in the amount of time spent on Pretend play in the two cultural groups, with the Euro-American children spending more time on this activity. In addition, boys were seen to spend more time than girls in Constructive play ($p < .05$; boys average = 3.1 *vs*. 1.7 for girls).

Finally, there was a significant interaction of Culture and Age on the amount of time children played Board Games or Puzzles ($p < .01$), indicating that at the older age Euro-American pre-schoolers were doing more constructive play the Asian children. There were no significant main effects or interactions for Simple Social play or Organized Sports and Lessons (see Table 6.5).

We further examined the subcategories of the kinds of pre-academic activities these children partook in (recall that the Asian children spent more time on pre-academic activities in general). Univariate ANOVAs carried out for five kinds of learning activities showed significant cultural differences for each one, although the differences were not uniformly in the same direction: Asian children spent more time on learning letters and numbers, learning early math skills, playing alphabet and number games, and playing and learning computers. By contrast, the Euro-American children spent more time reading books at bedtime. The magnitude of these differences was quite striking, for example, the Asian children were spending over 1 hour weekly learning early math skills, compared to only about 7 minutes for the Euro-American children. Overall, the Asian children were spending about 5 hours and 45 minutes weekly on the first four activities combined, compared to about 1 hour 40 minutes for the Euro-American children. On the other hand, as noted earlier, the Euro-American children were being read books at bedtime more frequently, about 4 hours weekly on average, compared to just under 3 hours for the Asian children.

Teachers' Ratings and Observations

Given the pervasive cultural differences between the Asian and Euro-American parents' ideas and practices related to children's play and learning, one might ask how these differences at home might influence children's behaviour at pre-school. Although we did not have any direct observational measures of the children in this setting, teachers' responses on the Child's Behaviour Inventory of Playfulness provide evidence on their perceptions of the child at school. The teachers' responses to this questionnaire were analyzed in a three-way MANOVA (Culture × Sex × Age). No significant main effects or interactions were found on the children's overall playfulness.

In addition to this questionnaire, however, ten of the teachers were interviewed about their impressions of the Asian children by comparison with the Euro-American children, and here some differences did emerge. Not surprisingly, the teachers reported that the Asian children had greater competence in letters and numbers when they first arrived at school. Interestingly, the teachers also commented that the Asian children tended at first to choose art work or quiet activities during free playtime. Asian children were also described as less aggressive, less complaining, and more likely to withdraw from situations where there were arguments or disagreements. All these differences, however, are said to disappear over time as the children settled into the school routines. One teacher commented, "Oh, my! Asian kids when they first arrive in pre-school, already know their letters and numbers. I don't know what their parents are doing at home. Asian kids are quiet and less aggressive, and they complain less when other children hit them. They just smile and get away. They also do not use the words 'thank you,' 'excuse me' and 'sorry', a lot.' But soon they learn to be like any other preschooler in the class." One pre-school director summarized: "Asian kids are very quiet in the classroom settings. I think their parents are very pushy at home and also they have very high expectations from their pre-schoolers, which I do not think does any good, but we help them to be themselves here."

Discussion

The present research demonstrates the cultural basis of beliefs and practices relevant to early childhood education in the Euro-American and Asian cultures. There are two contrasting patterns of beliefs and practices. As anticipated, the Euro-American parents believed play to be an important vehicle for the early development and growth of the pre-school children. They considered play helpful in enhancing physical, social, emotional and cognitive development. In contrast, the Asian parents did not value play for the development of preschool children. They did not believe play helps children get ready for school. The Asian parents stressed the idea that getting a head start in early academics is important for the cognitive development of children in the pre-school years.

There was one unanticipated cultural difference in parental thinking, given the evidence that Asian parents demand more obedience or compliance from their children (Liu, 1986): the Asian parents here scored lower than Euro-American parents on the Compliance Sub-Scale of the Education Attitude Scale. A closer examination of the compliance items of the Educational Attitude Scale, however, suggests it assesses a limited range of behaviours: 'saying please and thank you' or 'trying new foods.' These behaviours may reflect specific, culturally defined polite behaviour rather than compliance even for American pre-school children. The Asian children did not use these terms at home, because, as one Asian parent explained, these terms are for respect outside the family, and to use them at home would imply the children were somehow not part of the family. It was evident from the teachers' interviews that Asian children do not use these polite words when they first arrive in pre-school settings. They learn to say 'thank you' and 'sorry' only after they start their Euro-American preschool.

Cultural differences in parents' culturally shared beliefs about play and learning were instantiated in practices at home related to provision of toys, organization of the home for play and learning, and the use of time. The Euro-American parents believed play to be an important vehicle for young children's academic and social development and therefore, provided far more resources in terms of the number of toys, especially those that were simply for fun and enjoyment. In contrast, the Asian parents bought fewer toys, and those they selected were more typically educational toys. Euro-American parents facilitated their children's play by playing with their children themselves, whereas the Asian parents facilitated cognitive development by serving as teachers and academic coaches at home.

The constellation of related beliefs and practices described in this research provides an example of how the child's culturally structured developmental niche organizes the child's experiences and opportunities for learning over the course of development. As Super and Harkness (1999) have suggested, it is the redundancy among different components of the niche—parental ethnotheories, physical and social settings of daily life, and customs and practices of care—that provides the special power of cultural effects on development. Elaborated over time and across settings, these cultural differences in the developmental niches of children can have profound influences on the development of competence.

The present research has documented two contrasting sets of culturally based experience for young children. One is based on Euro-American ethnotheories, and is shared by the Euro-American parents and the Euro-American preschool teachers; for the Euro-American children, this overlap provides the kind of redundancy that is to be expected across settings within a single culture. The Asian parents hold to different ethnotheories, and thus for the Asian children, the developmental niches of home and school were discordant in important ways. In general, US society has favored "stimulation," advancement, and the maximization of children's individual potential; thus it is noteworthy that a cultural group that would appear to out-perform even the most competitive middle-class parents elicited the disapproval of teachers. The Asian children all appeared to be making a good adjustment to school, but the teacher-parent disagreement can presage problems for programmes for culturally divergent populations; the preschool is in effect a cultural intervention. As Harkness and Super (1993, p. 130) have written, "Children's culturally structured learning experiences are set within a larger framework of daily life that is also organized by parents. Successful interventions with families, thus, need to incorporate a re-examination of cultural belief systems and their customary expression in the institutions that serve those families, as well as in the families themselves, so that beliefs and practices through out the child's developmental niche can support and enhance each other."

In a multi-cultural society like the modern US, there are many challenges for parents and teachers in understanding and bridging the differences in ethnotheories. All over the world, with increased levels of travel and immigration, many countries are becoming more culturally diverse. The change in the US is particularly profound: no other nation comprises such a culturally diverse population. School policies, educational institutions, and teachers need to be sensitive to cultural diversity. When children come from cultural backgrounds in which their parents have different educational and socialization goals from those offered by Euro-American school settings, confusion and conflict will naturally sometimes result. It seem elemental that, under these circumstances, both teachers and parents understand the cultural nature of their own beliefs about early development, as well as the others', and strive to resolve them in ways beneficial to the child.

REFERENCES

Chao, R.K. (1996). Chinese and Euro-American mother's beliefs about the role of parenting in children's school success. *Journal of Cross-cultural Psychology, 27* (4), 403-423.

Chao, R.K. (2000). In R.D. Taylor & M.C. Wang (Eds.), *Resilience across contexts: Family, work, culture, and community,* pp. 333-363. Mahwah, NJ, Lawrence Erlbaum Associates, Inc.

Chen, C. & Stevenson, H.W. (1995). Motivation and mathematics achievement: A comparative study of Asian-American, Caucasian-American, and East Asian high school students. *Child Development, 66* (4), 1215-1234.

Farver, J. A.M. (1999). Activity setting analysis: A model for examining the role of culture in development. In A. Göncü (Ed.), *Children's Engagement in the World: Sociocultural perspectives* (pp. 99-127). Cambridge: Cambridge University Press.

Farver, J.A.M., & Howes, C. (1993). Cultural differences in American and Mexican mother-child pretend play. *Merrill-Palmer Quarterly, 39*(3), 344-358.

Farver, J.A.M. & Wimbarti, S. (1995). Indonesian children's play with their mothers. *Child Development. 66*, 1493-1503.

Farver, J.A.M., Kim, Y.K., & Lee, Y. (1995). Cultural differences in

Korean and Anglo-American preschoolers' social interaction and play behaviors. *Child Development, 66*, 1088-1099.

Gaskins, S. (1999). Children's daily lives in a Mayan village: A case study of culturally constructed roles and activities. In A. Göncü (Ed.), *Children's Engagement in the World: Sociocultural perspectives* (pp. 25-61). Cambridge: Cambridge University Press.

Goodnow, J.J., Miller, P.J. & Kessel, F. (Eds.) (1995). *Cultural practices as contexts for development*. New Directions for Child Development Vol. 67. San Francisco: Jossey-Bass.

Harkness, S. & Super, C.M. (1992). From parents' cultural belief systems to behavior. *In* L. Eldering & P. Leseman (Eds.), *Effective early intervention: Cross-cultural perspectives*, pp. 67-90. New York: Falmer Press.

Harkness, S. & Super, C.M. (1999). Parental ethnotheories in action. *In* I. E. Sigel, A. V. McGillicuddy-DeLisi, & J. J. Goodnow (Eds.), *Parental belief systems: The psychological consequences for children*, Second Edition, pp. 373-391. Hillsdale, N. J.: L. Erlbaum Associates.

Harkness, S. & Super, C.M. (Eds.) (1996). *Parents' cultural belief systems: Their origins, expressions, and consequences*. New York: Guilford.

Harkness, S., & Super, C.M. (1986). The cultural structuring of children's play in a rural African community. In K. Blanchard (Ed.), *The Many Faces of play* (pp. 96-103). Champaign, IL: Human Kinetics.

Harkness, S., & Super, C.M. (1993). The developmental niche: Implications for children's literacy development. In L. Eldering & P. Leseman, (Eds.), *Early intervention and culture: Preparation for literacy* (pp. 115-132). Paris: UNESCO.

Harkness, S., Hughes, M., Muller, B., & Super, C. M. (In press). Entering the developmental niche: Mixed methods in an intervention program for inner-city children. In T. Weisner (Ed.), *Discovering successful pathways in children's development: Mixed methods in the study of childhood and family life.*

Hollingshead, A.B. (1975). *Four factor index of social status*. Unpublished manuscript, Yale University.

Huntsinger, C.S., Jose, P.E., Liaw, F.R., & Ching, W.D. (1997). Cultural differences in early mathematics learning: A comparison of Euro-American, Chinese-American, and Taiwan-Chinese Families. *International Journal of Behavioral Development, 21*, 371-388.

Lightfoot, C. & Valsiner, J. (1992). Parental belief systems under the influence: Social guidance of the construction of personal cultures. In I.E. Siegel, A.V. McGillicuddy DeLisi, & J. Goodnow (Eds.),

Parental Belief Systems: The psychological consequences for children. Hillsdale, NJ: Erlbaum.

Liu, W.T. (1986). Culture and social support. *Research on Aging, 8* (1), 57-83.

Piaget, J. (1962). *Play, Dreams, and Imitation in Childhood.* New York: Norton.

Rescorla, L. (1991). Parent and teacher attitudes about early academics. In L. Rescorla, M. Hyson, K. Hirsh-Pasek, & J. Cone (Eds.), *Academic instruction in early childhood: Challenge or pressure?* New Directions for Child Development, *53.* San Francisco: Jossey-Bass.

Rogers, C.S., Impara, J.C., Frary, R.B., Harris, T., Meeks, A., Semanic-Lauth, S., & Reynolds, M. R. (1998). Measuring playfulness: Development of the Child Behavior Inventory of Playfulness. *Play and Culture, 4,* 121-135.

Rogoff, B., Mistry, J., Göncü, A. & Mosier, C. (1993). Guided participation in cultural activity by toddlers and caregivers. *Monographs* of the Society for Research in Child Development, 236, (58-8).

Roopnarine, J.L., Johnson, J., & Hooper, F. (1994). *Children's Play in Diverse Cultures.* Albany: State University of New York Press.

Roopnarine, J.L., Lasker, J., Sacks, M., & Stores, M. (1998). The cultural context of children's play. In O. N. Saracho and B. Spodek (Eds.). *Multiple Perspectives on Play in Early Childhood Education,* pp.194-219, Albany: State University of New York Press.

Schwartzman, H.G. (1978). *Transformations: The Anthropology of Play.* New York: Plenum.

Stevenson, H.W, Lee, S.-Y., Chen, C., & Stigler, J.W. (1990). Contexts of achievement: A study of American, Chinese, and Japanese children. *Monographs* of the Study for Research in Child Development, *55* (1-2).

Stevenson, H.W., Lee, S.-Y., Chen, C., & Lummis, M. (1990). Mathematics achievement of children in China and the United States. *Child Development, 61*(4), 1053-1066.

Super, C.M. & Harkness, S. (1999). The environment as culture in developmental research. In T. Wachs & S. Friedman (Eds.) *Measurement of the environment in developmental research,* pp. 279-323. Washington, DC: American Psychological Association.

Vygotsky, L.S. (1976). Play and its role in emotional development. In J. S. Bruner, A. Jolly, & K. Sylva (Eds.), *Play: Its role in development and evolution,* pp. 537-544, New York: Basic Books.

Vygotsky, L.S. (1978). *Mind in Society.* Cambridge, MA: Harvard University Press.

Wachs, T. & Friedman, S. (Eds.) (1999). *Measurement of the environment in developmental research.* Washington, DC: American Psychological Association.

Whiting, B.B., & Edwards, C.P. (1988). *Children of different worlds: The formation of social behavior*. Cambridge, Mass.: Harvard University Press.

7

Early Childhood Education in India from 1830s to 1940s: Leapfrogging Through a Century

BALJIT KAUR

> "It is one of the many consequences of the general lack of educational planning in India that a very impressionable plastic and educationally potent period of a child's life has received so little attention.... Outside India the nursery school has come into its own and has taken a well-defined place in the fabric of public instruction, but the importance of looking after the physical and mental welfare of future citizens from their earliest years has still to be brought home to the responsible authorities in this country. Official neglect, however, is far from being the only obstacle; ignorance and indifference on the part of the people most closely concerned has also contributed to the present sorry state of affairs. Even if proper facilities were provided, it would be by no means an easy matter to persuade the Indian mother to subordinate her natural affections in the interest of a more healthy physical and mental environment for her children. A great deal of propaganda and training of public opinion will be necessary before a system of pre-primary education can be successfully introduced." (Bureau of Education India 1944; p. 15)

These opening sentences of the chapter on Pre-Primary Education of the Report of Central Advisory Board on Post-

War Educational Development in India (Bureau of Education, 1944) under the chairmanship of Sargeant, have more than any other single official document shaped the widely accepted perceptions of early childhood education (ECE) in independent India. The report, 'the first one to devote a separate chapter' on preschool education, has been cited time and again by ECE professionals to reiterate that there was little or no provision for ECE in India prior to the turn of the 20th century, at which point some pre-schools were started by Scottish missionaries. In this chapter, I will outline a few selected developments in ECE during a century leading up to the Sargeant report and examine some of the reasons that could help us understand why this history of ECE has largely remained unclaimed and undocumented and the effects that such neglect might have on our current understandings.

A close reading of the above statement makes at least two claims evident. First, we are told that the government as well as public have been ignorant, neglectful and indifferent to the significance of educational input for young children. Second, the Indian public, particularly mothers, did not want to send their children to an educational institution given their emotional attachment with young children. Both these points are true in one reading of the statement. Despite the presence now of a very large ICDS provision and ever increasing number of private preschools, it can be argued that the Indian governments have not given adequate importance to ECE. That is as true of the independent India as it was of the colonial rulers. Similarly, a wide section of society does consider the family as the ideal context for young children's development and learning. While the ECE provisions have burgeoned in the last two or three decades or so, it is by no means universally accepted or preferred option even though a large majority of families now-a-days use it.

And yet, neither of the claims is true to the extent that it could apply to the entire country in such sweeping terms that little or no provision for ECE might have existed prior to the independence of India and that even if such provision had existed, families would not have taken advantage of it to educate their young children. If that were the case, it will be hard, for instance, to understand why Montessori's training courses in 1940s were so popular that women and men in hundreds travelled across long distances despite poor modes of transport year after year to attend them. The fact is that by the time Montessori arrived in India in 1939, the history of ECE in the country was already over a century old. She did not arrive in a country that was ignorant or indifferent to the idea of sending young children to an educational institution. No doubt, the actual number of children who availed of ECE was small, but the history of this provision cannot be denied on that count. By such an argument, college education too would have no history to claim in India prior to the turn of the century. And yet, we will be quick to realise the fallacy of such a position. My interest, then, lies in exploring the reasons for the relative disinterest in the history of early childhood education that has prevailed in India.

The Forgotten History

Selected Developments in ECE Prior to 1944

As elaborated elsewhere (Kaur, 2004), the start of ECE in India can be traced to the establishment of infant schools in the Presidency of Bengal and dates back to 1830, parallel to and influenced by similar developments in Europe, particularly England. Not only at the start but throughout this history, the provisions for ECE in India were influenced by and reflected the major trends in Europe, be it the establishment of infant schools or infant standards in primary schools, Froebel inspired Kindergartens or Montessori schools (For instance, see Whitbread, 1975; Beatty, 1995; May, 1997, 2005; Prochner, 2004). I will briefly outline some of the main developments in India, along with these parallels in Europe, mostly in England.

The most well known experiment in the education of young children in Europe has been that by a Welsh businessman, Robert Owen (1771-1858). He started his first infant school in

1816 in New Lenark, Scotland. Owen had a utopian vision of a New World in which education was to be the main harbinger of social and moral change. He wanted children as soon as they could walk, to attend what he called preparatory standards. Children between two and six years of age attended two such standards at New Lenark. Children could start as early as 18 months of age, literally as soon as they could walk. The reason for bringing children at such a young age under the influence of an institution was integrally tied to his utopian vision. Owen believed that the world could be rid of unhappiness, misery and crime if his method was followed to mould the next generation. In his words, "... the new system is founded on principles which will enable mankind to *prevent*, in the rising generation, almost all, if not all of the evils and miseries which we and our forefathers have experienced" (p. 108, emphasis in original). His principles included the following:

1. No scolding or punishment of the children.
2. Unceasing kindness in tone, look, word, and action, to all the children without exception...
3. Instruction by the inspection of realities and their qualities, ...and the taught... always allowed to ask their own questions ...
4. These questions to be always answered in a kind and rational manner; and when beyond the teacher's knowledge...at once to be fully admitted, so as never to lead the young mind into error.
5. No regular indoor hours for school: but the teachers to discover when the minds of the taught or their own minds, commenced to be fatigued by the indoor lesson, and then to change it for out-of-door physical exercise...
6. ... taught and exercised in military discipline, to teach them habits of order, obedience, and exactness, to improve their health and carriage, and to prepare them at the best time, in the best manner, when required, to defend their country at the least expense and trouble to themselves.
7. But these exercises to be continued no longer than they

were useful and could be beneficially enjoyed by the taught.

8. To take the children out to become familiar with the productions of gardens, orchards, fields, and woods, and with the domestic animals and natural history generally, is an essential part of the instruction to be given to the children of the working classes; and this was the practice in my time with the children at New Lanark. (pp. 175-176) (Harrison, 1968)

However, this was not the vision that prompted those who started infant schools in India, even though many of the practices advocated by Owen were prevalent in ECE centres of that time and even today. Instead, it was the influence of a contemporary of Owen, Samuel Wilderspin (1792-1866) that shaped the nature of infant schools in this country.

The fourth Bishop of Calcutta, Bishop Turner, started an infant school in 1830, in all probability the first such institution in British India. Thus, the widely held belief that it was the missionaries who started ECE in India is correct although it happened seven decades prior to the commonly accepted 'turn of the century'. The children attending this infant school were largely from Christian persuasion, whether of Indian or English origin. The British government's General Committee of Public Instruction, however, sanctioned an infant school that opened at Hoogly in 1839, which contrary to the common beliefs, then as now, was mostly attended by children from higher caste Hindu and other well-to-do families (General Committee of Public Instruction, 1842). The Hoogly infant school functioned successfully for 12 years before being closed, because by then "there were sufficient number of infant schools in the area" (General Committee of Public Instruction, 1851).

The idea to start an infant school at Hoogly was first mooted in 1836 by the principal of the newly opened Hoogly College, Dr. Wise, in his first annual report to the General Committee. However, Lord Macaulay the then Chair of the General Committee was opposed to the idea and stalled it for three years. Macaulay's minutes make an interesting reading on the debate between the members of the General Committee on both sides of the argument. The infant school could be opened finally only after Macaulay was no longer the chair (Kaur 2004). Boys as young as 3 or 3 and-a-half years and up to the age of 7 years were sent by their families to learn along the lines promoted for infant schools at that time. The primary schools, specially meant for Christian and British children included infant classes and admitted children between 3 and 4 years of age. However, the education of young children was not restricted to these populations. Throughout the century, one can find frequent, though fleeting, references to the existence of infant schools in the British territories and it is clear that such schools and classes were not catering only for the European children.

Samuel Wilderspin's objective was to save the children of the poor from a life of petty crime, and to do so efficiently and cost-effectively. Religious knowledge and inculcation of morals and values based on "the pure and perfect morality of the Scriptures" were the core of his infant education. He assiduously publicised the efficiency and cost effectiveness of his system. The 1823 edition of his popular book on Infant Education was subtitled, "Showing How Three Hundred Children from Eighteen Months to Seven Years of Age may be Managed by One Master and Mistress" (Beatty, 1995). This model of moral rescue and efficiency held huge appeal for missionaries and government alike in colonies like India as the archival records bear ample testimony (for instance, see Missionary Register, 1835).

By mid-nineteenth century, Friedrich Froebel's (1782-1852) ideas had been introduced into England, with the establishment of the first Kindergarten in London in 1851, and the Froebel movement was at its peak there around 1880s. This no doubt had an impact on the Indian scene. The most active and far-reaching changes were initiated in the 1880s in the Madras Presidency. In 1885, the Madras Presidency implemented a revised Grant–in–aid Code instituting an infant standard, which meant that infant classes were attached to all primary schools. Further, Froebel's Object Lessons and Kindergarten Occupations appear to be the most common 'subjects' introduced into the lower primary curriculum under the revised code, along with drawing, action songs and stories. (Duncan, 1887)

One significant consequence of that policy was the beginning of a dedicated kindergarten teacher training course in the late 1880s, arguably the first of its kind, at the Saidapet Teachers' College, Madras. Isabel Brander, a school inspectress who was a member of the committee that recommended the mandatory inclusion of infant classes in Madras, wrote one of the earliest books on Indian Kindergarten in 1899. A vernacular translation of the book was introduced within a year, in the hope that it will help in improved teacher training. Two of the staff members from the Kindergarten Department at the Saidapet College, Carol Gillingham and Corrie Gordon, also went on to write a number of books on the practice, principles and materials for Indian Kindergarten in early 20th century. This period of policy driven changes in infant education set the stage for a fairly active period at the turn of the century, not only in Madras but in virtually all the British territories, as evident from the 1904 education policy and the annual reports on Progress of Education in India of the time.

It is scarcely known in the field of ECE today that the British education policy in India, since the last quarter of the nineteenth century, advocated for the implementation of Kindergarten method in lower primary schools, particularly in the Infant, First and Second Standards. Kindergarten Occupations and Object Lessons were offered by a large number of children in these Standards all over the British territories. For example, the fourth quinquennial review reports that,

> "The three lowest classes of the new Bengal primary course are styled the infant classes. In these classes children are to be taught largely by the kindergarten method. The course includes kindergarten occupations, the alphabet and spelling book, writing words, the simple rules of European and native arithmetic, drawing—beginning with lines and ending with simple free-hand drawing and tracing, simple action songs, and elementary drill and gymnastics. " (p.161) (Nathan, 1903).

The report for the Bombay Presidency for the same period as above documents the changes effected there, indicating the extension of the Kindergarten methods into primary classes.

> "In the higher standards provision has been made for the teaching of Kindergarten occupations, object lessons, drill and gymnastic, singing, mensuration, instruction in simple agriculture and science, drawing and manual training. The Rural Standards contain the same preparation in the infant class, and thenceforward are specially devoted to the three R's, while particular attention is paid to native accounts, simple forms of agreement, the plants and animals of the locality, its agricultural productions, in addition to an elementary knowledge of sanitation. The masters are specially prepared in the Training Colleges in accordance with these alterations, and the Assistant Deputy Inspectors are also temporarily attached to these Colleges in order that they may fully understand what is expected from masters and pupils." (p.42) (1902)

Similarly, the Baroda Administration Reports for the years 1904 -1907 make references, albeit fleetingly, that infant schools existed in the State and that the Kindergarten method was adopted in primary schools, presumably in the lower three grades, which around that time comprised the compulsory years of schooling. However, the reason for starting separate infant schools might not find favour with the proponents of the education of the young today.

> " To reduce the burden of maintaining unwieldy primary classes in large towns and villages, the Departmental Rules enjoin the opening of Infant Schools wherever a teacher comes forward to teach little children in the First Standard and Below Standard classes. Nine such schools were maintained during the year under report; eight of them in the Baroda District." (pp. 218-219) (Dutt 1906)

Thus, the progress reports provide evidence for wide spread existence of infant classes as the first year of primary schools as well as strident advocacy for the introduction of Kindergarten method in lower primary standards in various provinces, accompanied by teacher training in the new methods at a number of places. The Girgaum Kindergarten Normal Class for its two-year training followed the course prescribed by the National Froebel Union in England (1908). The primary school in Bombay Presidency at this time had eight standards including the infant class.

Despite all this activity, the pedagogical ideas for infant classes were highly contested in India and this widespread opposition, in part resulted in undermining and reversing the earlier gains. The philosophy and pedagogy of Kindergarten never took root in the Indian soil. The paucity of adequately trained teachers and the lack of understanding of the spirit of Kindergarten method among teachers and public alike were lamented repeatedly by many educators, officials and inspectors.

The early 20th century was witness to the rise of child study movement, the scientific study of the psychological child, as well as Maria Montessori's (1870-1952) ideas about early education. Both of these new ideas were to have enormous impact on the education of young children throughout this century. The needs of children as related to different ages and stages of development came to be seen as important for making educational decisions. The implications of these new ways of thinking have been far reaching.

Gijubhai Badheka (1885-1939) almost single-handedly interpreted and implemented Montessori's ideas in the Indian context. His work at Dakshina Murti in Bhavnagar is well known in the ECE circles. He has been rightly credited to be a genuine pioneer in ECE in India although his work was concentrated in a relatively small geographic area, that is the western and north-western India. Gijubhai joined Dakshina Murti in 1916 as a teacher in the newly started primary school, Vinay Mandir. However, soon he started feeling that unless younger children got appropriate care and education, later schooling would have but superficial effects. So he proposed to start a Bal Mandir, an institution for young children's education, an initiative to which he devoted the rest of his life. Gijubhai's work during the next two decades was to wield a lasting influence on the field of ECE, directly through his experimentation for developing and adapting new methods for young children's education in India and indirectly through the professional training of hundreds of teachers, the establishment of the Montessori Sangh, and the publication of myriad materials for children, parents, and teachers.

In November 1926, Gijubhai organised a conference at Dakshina Murti, which served as a forum for wide ranging discussions in early education. More significantly, the conference resulted in the formation of the first 'Association of Pre-school Education' in India. The story of its name is an interesting one as recounted by Taraben (Modak, 1951). There was a detailed discussion about the name of the new association. Gijubhai wanted to call it the Montessori Shikshan Sangh, in order to honour his 'teacher', the inspiration behind his work on young children's education. The others had strong objections on various counts. First, this was the period of *Swadeshi* movement. National feelings were at the fore. At this time, to name the association after a foreigner was not acceptable to some members. Second, some members felt that there had to be freedom to try out any new ideas. By naming the association after one person, a misconception could be created that there was but one approach to be followed. They came up with several alternatives. However, Gijubhai believed that Montessori's work was meant for all children and she did not accept any distinctions or division. In the end, Gijubhai's plea was that he would feel he had failed in his duty as a 'student', if he did not pay adequate tribute and recognition to his 'teacher' on the day. Due to Gijubhai's unfailing devotion to his 'teacher', India was the first country to have a Montessori Association in this part of the world. His only concern seems to have been to 'free the children' using Montessori's principles. In light of such selfless devotion on his part, it is ironic that in later years Montessori was to doubt his intentions and suspect him of appropriating her name for his personal gain and fame. This is an interesting story though not within the scope of this chapter.

The members of the Sangh, particularly Gijubhai, were very proactive in recruiting new members. Gijubhai stipulated that the spouses had to join as individual members. Within one year the membership had exceeded 3,000 (1929). The members were widely spread in central, northern and western India. A large number were from Karachi at one end and Calcutta at the other. Some members were from other countries, Africa and European countries. Presumably due to the language barrier, the Sangh had little presence in the South, with only 9 members reported from Madras. (1929)

Since early 1939, it had been widely known that Madam Montessori was likely to visit India. Taraben (Modak, 1951) vividly recounts the excitement and devotion with which Gijubhai awaited the event. Such accounts might be responsible for the widely accepted misconception today that Gijubhai trained with Montessori during her visit to India. However, Gijubhai passed away in June 1939, just a few months before Montessori reached India. The two never met. He considered her his teacher because his practice was inspired by her ideas.

Montessori conducted a number of training courses during her first visit to India between 1939 and 1946 in various parts of India. The courses were incredibly popular and were attended by literally hundreds by women and men from across the Indian subcontinent, a fact well documented in the ECE literature.

The Missing Links

A Legacy of Neglect and Negation

In view of the commonly held beliefs to the contrary, evidence of a history as long and rich as that in Europe comes as somewhat of a surprise. Given the rough sketch of historical developments in the 100 years prior to the Sargeant report outlined above, the question of how to interpret the comments in that report gets sharpened. It is true that young children's education continues to be neglected in the official provision and policy.

However, it is equally true that the activity and provision of ECE in India has moved along similar lines and across comparable time frame as the Western world. Yet unlike the West, this history has not been systematically documented or claimed by the ECE professionals and researchers, and this neglect continues to shape the somewhat erroneous perceptions about the field of ECE in the country. For example, one reason for the continued neglect of ECE is seen to be the evolving phase of this 'young' sector of education (Viruru, 2001). In essence, the neglect is two-fold. First, ECE as a policy initiative or provision has never received due priority in education, even though its beginnings are as old in India as elsewhere in the world. Second, its history has not been studied adequately or systematically such that it could inform the current understandings about its status.

The contemporary published sources on ECE provide ample evidence that the study of the history of this field has not been a favourite topic for researchers. Although a few attempts have been made at some documentation, the picture particularly pertaining to the beginnings of ECE in India remains ambiguous at best. For instance, in the fourth and enlarged edition of his book, *History and philosophy of pre-primary and nursery education*, Aggarwal (1992) reiterated the pioneering role of Christian missionaries in introducing nursery education in India and made note of two important nursery schools started by missionaries, St. Hilda Infant School in Poona established in 1805 and Loreto Convent in Lucknow, established in 1874 (p. 127). Of all the materials published in relatively recent times that I have come across, this makes St. Hilda India's first school in the area of ECE. Fortunately, the school in question still exists in Pune. A visit to the school and examination of its history leaves no doubt that the school, which indeed had an infant section attached to it was started only in 1904, a century later than the starting date assigned to it by Aggarwal. In fact, the Sisters of the St. Mary the Virgin, who started the original St. Hilda School (called the Epiphany School at that time) with nursery and kindergarten in 1884 did not arrive in India till

December 1877. It was named St. Hilda School and set up as a girls' school in 1904 (St. Hilda School n.d.).

In the rest of this chapter, I will try to discuss some of the reasons for the prevailing neglect of the ECE and its history. Let me begin with a brief description of my engagement with the history of ECE. I do so in order to clarify my reasons for undertaking the task of setting some of the historical record straight.

For over a decade, I have been engaged in documenting a history of ECE in India. I am currently writing a book based on this research. The project that was originally expected to confine itself to a few interviews with ECE professionals has come to have a life of its own. My idea was very simple (and simplistic). I wanted to interview some of the eminent and/or long serving people in ECE to find out what their aspirations had been when they first started working in the field. How they had come to participate and what roles had they played? And what did they think of the changing face of ECE? The project over the years has received generous support from several former students and ex-colleagues. It has been an extremely rewarding, although time consuming and at times frustrating experience, in part because of faulty perceptions held by me and others, shaped by the erroneous, yet widely accepted information. The interviewees (as well as interviewers, in those cases where I could not conduct the interviews personally) were ECE professionals who had been involved in this field in some capacity for most of their working lives. During the course of conducting and/or transcribing more than seventy interviews, it became obvious to me that some things just did not work, in that there were too many gaps and contradictions in the oral histories for them to make a coherent narrative without extensive archival searches. This library work has been equally fascinating and has taken me to archives in several countries and across India.

One point I would like to emphasise is that the information that I am using to create a narrative of the history of ECE in India has all along been in the public arena. Some researcher, off and on, has stated some of it, albeit in passing. However, it is my contention that such information has not been taken to be a significant basis for a historical account that could anchor the field in the Indian education system in its due place.

The history of primary education and ECE is intertwined at various points in their history. Both can trace their roots to the same philosophical ideas and more or less same institutional structures. While in India, the indigenous schooling had an independent and long tradition, the beginnings of the Western type of schooling that is prevalent today lie in the same soil as those of the early childhood education. As is apparent from the brief outline presented above, through most of the 19th century, ECE initiatives were more often than not a part of the primary school. And yet, by early- to mid-twentieth century, a universal provision for primary school was being advocated assiduously while the pre-school went into plateau if not decline. I would argue that at least one of the main reasons of the latter's neglect lies in this relationship between pre-primary and primary education itself.

There appear to be at least two reasons for the official neglect of ECE; first, the perpetual inadequacy of funding for the expansion of primary schools at the required scale, and second, the prevailing understandings of the purposes of education at Primary and Early Childhood levels. The lack of funding has been a perennial problem for the primary education in India before and after Independence. As a consequence, the available funds do not stretch to lower ages. But, the funding has been only a part of the problem, arguably perhaps less central than the widely accepted beliefs about the purpose and meaning of education at the two levels.

In early twentieth century, nationalist leaders demanded free and compulsory primary education for the children of India in keeping with the overseas trends. Gopal Krishan Gokhale was one of the first and most vociferous advocates of this demand. In 1910 and again in 1911, he raised the issue in the Imperial Legislative Council to recommend the free and compulsory elementary education in the country. Although the motion was lost, his views were widely echoed in the country, particularly in the wake of the successful launch of free and compulsory education in the state of Baroda in 1906. As soon as education was devolved to the local governments in 1919, the Provinces one by one passed acts to mandate free and compulsory primary education. By 1930, all the Provinces in the British territory had agreed to provide free and compulsory primary education, even though the actual provision was nowhere near adequate for the population involved.

As J. P. Naik was to write decades later, Gokhale's primary emphasis had been on the hard task of convincing the rulers that there was a strong case for extending the primary education to the 'masses'. The related question, that of the administrative and financial implications of such a proposal, was not worked out by him at that time in any detail (Naik, 1976). It would seem that such details did not get their due from the Provincial governments either. The financial and administrative implications of this drive for mass elementary education paradoxically worked against the interests of Early Childhood Education. For instance, R. V. Parulekar, in suggesting ways of implementing this policy, recommended that the admission to elementary schools should be restricted to children of seven plus years of age, ostensibly to "reduce stagnation" in elementary school (Parulekar 1934; Parulekar 1939). The argument as detailed by another contemporary was that,

> Children are admitted to school at very tender ages. They soon find the class-room completely dry and uninteresting and fail to follow the teacher, the result being that they either remain in the same class for two or more years or leave the school never to return. It is a tremendous waste of public money to admit under-aged pupils to schools when their minds are not receptive to learning. (p. 42) (Desai, 1938)

A number of points made in this statement have a bearing on my argument. Educationists and leaders arguing for 'at least basic literacy skills for all children' were well intended as far as their goal of liberating the masses of India from illiteracy was concerned. They saw it as their paramount objective. Leaders like Gokhale knew the economic constraints of the system thus did not aim at any higher skills, settling for only four years of compulsion. These four years were to be devoted at creating literate masses, who could participate in the social and political life of the nation. These were serious objectives, philosophically in line with the way schooling has traditionally been seen in India. There was no place for wasting the precious resources. They wanted to ensure that the educational provision would be maximally utilised. The question of who should be entitled to attend these elementary classes thus became a matter of considerable importance. At least two sources of information were available at the time that could help them decide the issue. One source came from the Child Study movement. Psychology through systematic child study had newly acquired 'scientific' information based on 'objective observations' and 'tests' about the nature, needs and capabilities of the child at various age-related stages. This information told them that children below seven years of age were not capable of benefiting from schooling.

> "[T]o admit infants below the age of seven to ordinary schools will only result in more harm than good. We, therefore, suggest that no child should be admitted to a primary school before he completes his seventh year and that the present lower limit of compulsion in various provinces should be raised to seven years." (p. 41) (Desai, 1938)

Consonant with the information from child psychology, a number of educators had been writing about the special pedagogy appropriate for Kindergartens and nursery schools. The young children were not to be given formal instruction in the 3 Rs. Their education must be based on activity, creativity, and fun for them so that they will come to enjoy schooling. Although this 'new method', as it was referred to, was supposed to be appropriate for the lower primary grades also, this idea had never been fully accepted in India. Seven year olds entering elementary school were thought to be capable of undertaking the responsibility of learning the basic skills, undeterred by the 'dull and uninteresting class-room', and to fulfil the dreams of a literate nation.

The incompatibility between the meanings attached to the two levels of education is clear. By this time in India, as in Western countries, separate Kindergartens, nursery schools or infant sections attached to schools were not uncommon. This latter reality made it easier for educators to think separately about the 'pre-schools', which were somewhat trivial in the face of the real task of eradicating illiteracy associated with the elementary schools.

> "It is no doubt desirable to have infant schools where children under seven can enjoy happy and homely surroundings. Such of the provincial Governments who can find money to maintain infant schools in addition to primary schools for the whole school-going population should certainly do so. But at the same time, it would be wrong to open infant schools when the greater need of the country in maintaining primary schools is not fully satisfied." (p. 40) (Desai, 1938)

Kindergartens, thus, were seen to be a luxury, a trivial institution for those countries (and provinces) who had plenty of resources, not for India engaged as it was with the most onerous task of reconstruction of the society through education. Early Childhood Education was never seen to be integral to the efforts that India launched throughout the twentieth century to attain the dream of universal elementary education. The Zakir Hussain Committee in 1937 also recommended seven *plus* as the starting point for compulsory elementary education, lamenting the paucity of finances.

> "We realise that by fixing seven plus as the age for introduction of compulsory education, we have left out a very important period of child's life to be shaped in the rather unfavourable surroundings of poor village home under the care of uneducated and indifferent parents mostly struggling against unbearable circumstances. We feel very strongly the necessity for some organisation of

> preschool education conducted or supported by the State, for children between the ages of three and seven. A painful consciousness of the realities of the situation, chiefly financial, prevents us from making this recommendation." (p. 36) (Zakir Hussain Committee, 1938)

Even an eminent educationist like Dr. J. P. Naik, despite his unfailing advocacy in favour of children and his generous patronage of the Indian Association of Preschool Education, does not seem to be consistently concerned about the education for the younger child in particular. In 1976, his comment on Parulekar's recommendation for restricting elementary education to seven plus was that it was a new proposal, which "has a bias in favour of mass education but is unpalatable to the classes whose one ambition is to send their children to school at increasingly lower ages". (p. 18) (Naik, 1976)

Education for the younger children has not been on the agenda of the Departments of Education in Indian universities either. The Departments of Education consider it their business to study and teach at all levels of education including non-formal adult education, except the pre-school education. It could be argued that this reflects the tension between the primary and pre-school education. Perhaps the professionals in education are themselves not convinced about the importance of pre-school education. The early childhood education - the need for it, the approaches to it - has derived its force from sources largely outside the discipline of education as practised in the departments of education in the country. As such, it has not benefited from being a part of an Arts and Social Sciences faculty with a convention of historical study and research. The focus has been on the professional development of ECE workers rather than on a study of the field from a particular stance - be it historical, sociological, economic and so forth. Further, a historical account of ideas is likely to be a focal point of inquiry in a well-established area, since such research constitutes a deliberate consideration of the accepted wisdom, a 'looking back to take stock'. It is less likely to happen if the independent status of the field itself is in doubt.

ECE has only been a subsidiary occupation of the Child Development Departments in Faculties of Home Science. A number of aspects of the structural placement of ECE in Home Science are interesting. Home Science was traditionally seen to be education appropriate for girls of well-to-do families to teach them the art and craft of managing a home better once they got married. To a large extent the same public perception prevails even today with minor modifications. No men seek admission in Home Science Colleges, although the admission is open to any one, and hardly any men teach in one, particularly not in the Departments of Child Development. The unspoken relationship between the societal role of women and young children's care and education might lie at the core of this arrangement, with its attendant marginalising effects for the field of ECE. On their part, almost all Child Development Departments have an experimental nursery school but few concern themselves with the education of the child beyond that age. There are no experimental primary schools attached to any of the Departments of Child Development.

Surely Child Development is as relevant an influence for the education of children beyond six, as it is for those below six. There seems to be a clear divide between the Departments of Education and the Departments of Child Development. Each remains largely unaware of the work done by the other. Two questions arise from this situation: Why has such a division arisen? What are the implications of this divide for the education of children?

This divide and its implications or reasons have seldom been noticed or questioned. A rare exception was an exchange between Vinod Raina and S. Anandalaksmy at New Delhi in 1996 at a panel discussion hosted by the Lady Irwin College of Home Science. Raina was of the view that curriculum development for primary school requires input and support from Child Development. In response Anandalakshmy accepted that the Child Development had not focused on the education of the children above the pre-school age. The reasons, she said, lie partly in the American system of attaching laboratory pre-schools to the Child Development Departments that has been continued unquestioned in India. But Child Development has not had impact on pre-school curriculum across the board either. "The real reason is that the people from Child Development become powerless in front of people who decide what textbooks should have and what curriculum should be formed" (p. 67) (Chaudhary, 1996). Unfortunately, the question as to why the Education Departments did not consider Early Childhood Education an integral part of their professional responsibility was not raised.

As we have seen earlier, there was little institutional or structural division between the pre-school and primary school till early 20th century. The calls for free and compulsory primary education on the one hand and the 'scientific' knowledge about children's age and stage based needs and competencies on the other, gave rise to the need to mandate the age limits, arguably to the detriment of the education of the children below six or seven years of age. The reasons were stated to be economic, although that is not the whole story.

The policy makers, politicians and the general public have for different reasons contributed to the neglect that early childhood education has suffered over time, and arguably, continues to suffer today. The professionals in education and child development have compounded this neglect by ignoring the study of history of ECE. History tells us that the issues facing the field today are not new. Perhaps more awareness of the beliefs that have shaped the decision-making in the past can guard against the some of the pitfalls ahead. Hopefully, this brief historical sketch will serve as an invitation to fellow researchers to further this discussion by looking closely at the history of ECE in India.

REFERENCES

Beatty, B. (1995). *Preschool education in America: The culture of young children from the colonial era to the present.* New Haven, Yale University Press.

Bureau of Education India (1944). *Post-war educational development in*

India. Report by the Central Advisory Board of Education. Delhi, Manager of Publications.

Chaudhary, N. (1996). *Meeting the needs of the child in India: Challenges to the Child Development professional.* Silver Jubilee Celebrations of the Department of Child Development. New Delhi, Lady Irwin College.

Desai, D.D. (1938). *Primary education in India.* Bombay, Servants of India Society.

Duncan, D. (1887). *Report on Public Instruction in the Madras Presidency for 1885-1886.* Madras, Government of India.

Dutt, R.C. (1906). *Baroda Adminstration Report 1904-05.* Printed at Bombay: The British India Printing Works. Baroda, The State of Baroda.

General Committee of Public Instruction (1842). *Report of Public Instruction for 1840-41 & 1841-42.* Calcutta, William Rushton & Co.

General Committee of Public Instruction (1851). *Report on Public Instruction in the Lower Provinces 1849-1850.* Calcutta, Public Instruction in the Lower Provinces of The Bengal Presidency 1 October 1849 to 30 September 1850.

Harrison, J. F. C., Ed. (1968). Utopianism and education: *Robert Owen and the Owenites*. Classics in Education. New York, Teachers' College Press.

Kaur, B. (2004). "'Keeping the infants of coolies out of harm's way': Raj, Church, and Infant Education in India 1830-1851." *Contemporary Issues in Early Childhood, 5*(3), 221-235.

May, H. (1997). *The discovery of early childhood: The development of services for the care and education of very young children - Mid eighteenth century Europe to mid-twentieth century New Zealand.* Auckland: Auckland University Press, Bridget Williams Books & New Zealand Council for Educational Research.

May, H. (2005). *School beginnings: A nineteenth century colonial story.* Wellington: New Zealand Council for Educational Research.

Missionary Register (1835). *Missionary Register for MDCCCXXXV : containing the principal transactions of the various institutions for propagating the Gospel: with the proceedings, at large, of the Church Missionary Society.* London: L. B. Seeley & Sons.

Modak, T. (1951). Nutan Bal Shikshan Sangh: An overview of 25 years. *Shikshan Patrika (Gujarati) 26*(3): 1-16.

Naik, J.P. (1976). *Elementary education in India: A promise to keep.* Bombay: Allied Publishers.

Nathan, R. (1903). *Progress of education in India 1897-98 - 1901-02 Fourth quinquennial review*. Office of the Director General of India.

Parulekar, R.V. (1934). *Mass education in India.* Bombay: Local Self Government Institute.

Parulekar, R.V. (1939). *Literacy in India.* Bombay: Macmillan & Co.

Prochner, L. (2004). Early childhood education programs for indigenous children in Canada, Australia and New Zealand: An historical overview, *Australian Journal of Early Childhood, 29* (4), 7-16.

Report of the Director of Public Instruction on Progress of Education in the Bombay Presidency during the Quinquennium from 1897-98 to 1901-02. 1902, Bombay, Government Central Press.

Report of the Director of Public Instruction on Progress of Education in the Bombay Presidency during the Quinquennium from 1902-03 to 1906-07. 1908, Bombay, Government Central Press.

Second Montessori Conference. *Shikshan Patrika (Gujarati), 4*(2 & 3), 1929, 18-31.

St. Hilda School (n.d.). *1877-1977 Centenary of the arrival of the community of St. Mary the Virgin to Panch Howd*, Poona. Pune: 7.

Viruru, R. (2001). *Early childhood education: Postcolonial perspectives from India.* New Delhi: Sage Publications.

Whitbread, N. (1975). *The evolution of the nursery-infant school: A history of infant and nursery education in Britain, 1800-1970.* London, Routledge & Kegan Paul.

Zakir Hussain Committee (1938). *Educational reconstruction.* Bombay, All India National Conference, Wardha.

8

Conclusion

PRERANA MOHITE and LARRY PROCHNER

Together, the chapters attempt to present a multidimensional nature of ECCE in India. Though the writings essentially focus on the India scenario, the concerns and issues that emerge in the field of ECCE may be applicable to several cultures and societies, especially in developing Afro-Asian countries. There are pertinent emerging themes that need to be understood and addressed.

Adequate body of knowledge about ECCE is now generated through researches, theories and time tested practices. The studies have contributed to knowledge about effective early learning, curriculum design, development and implementation, teacher knowledge, perception and behaviour, multifunctional early childhood services, policy development and several other crucial areas. This knowledge base provides insight into what early childhood educators and parents need to know and provide to children and families in the contemporary situation. Through wide dissemination of knowledge across countries, a broad based international perspective is created about nature of children's development and education.

Since researches have repeatedly provided evidences related to the long lasting significant influence of experiences in the early years to later development, the policy-makers have finally "taken note" of it. Consequently, one finds significant policy level awareness and development for early intervention programmes, especially as part of national level efforts to counteract the effects of adverse psychosocial and medical conditions in infancy and early childhood. In short, there is now "political will" to support and enhance early childhood education and development.

Through developments in the field of cross-cultural psychology, a clear cultural and ecological perspective is visible in the field, especially in developing nations. Relatively recently, education has shifted its thinking towards acknowledging the critical position of local settings and cultures in a number of ways in creating a context of human development.

The need to know, understand and preserve the "indigenous knowledge" is felt and acknowledged equally by developing and developed nations. Along this thinking and concept, there is also an acknowledgement of efforts towards interdisciplinary perspective across early childhood research, theoretical tenets and policy development. Interestingly, the need for indigenous knowledge and local experience representing Indian/any country's objectives also extend across cultures, including international trends and issues. The challenge for the field of ECCE is to develop a perspective that is locally rooted and globally relevant, as also to place research and theory in local context and develop culturally specific tools and strategies for research and theory building. Efforts to meet this challenge are reflected in several researches, theoretical advances and perspectives in the field of ECCE as some of the chapters included in this book indicate.

Stemming from such a perspective, yet another crucial issue and concern is: How to develop policies and programmes that represent harmonized linkages between local and global? How to design social programme strategies that affect the well-being of children and their families significantly and effectively? There are no easy answers to such challenges and questions, but it is heartening to note that increasingly, countries are investing in programmes for young children that are more holistic and integrated in nature. Increasingly, the programmes are based on sound research as well as theory and tested locally before scaling up. Though there are miles to go in this direction, one can certainly state that, the idea of reaching out to young children and their families in a holistic way is almost universally accepted.

Also, concerted efforts towards forging interface between research, policies and indigenous thoughts and practices are visible in conceptualization of research ideas, in theoretical concepts as well as in programme development and implementation. At the level of Government, it is becoming a common practice to consult researchers as well as practitioners in formulating polices and programmes. Therefore, it may be warranted to state that while the partnership needs to be strengthened, it certainly is no more an "uneasy" partnership. The field of ECCE is poised at an exciting point where disciplinary boundaries are getting diluted and concerted efforts towards building effective programmes are visible across countries resulting in a wide range of researches and programmes for young children, jointly conceived by government, NGOs and academic institutions. One hopes that concerted efforts across countries to provide a better life to children will certainly yield outcomes that we all are hoping for.

Index